In Honor of
Henry H. Mitchell

Preaching on the Brink

The Future of Homiletics

Martha J. Simmons

EDITOR

FOREWORD BY

Gardner Taylor

Abingdon Press

Nashville

PREACHING ON THE BRINK:
THE FUTURE OF PREACHING

Copyright © 1996 by Abingdon Press

This book is printed on recycled, acid-free paper.

Library of Congress Cataloging-in-Publication Data

Preaching on the brink : the future of preaching : in honor of Henry H. Mitchell / edited by Martha J. Simmons : foreword by Gardner Taylor.
   p. cm.
  Includes bibliographical references and index.
  ISBN 0-687-01154-X (pbk. : alk. paper)
  1. Preaching. I. Mitchell, Henry H. II. Simmons, Martha J.
BV4211.2.P73726 1996   96-17509
251—dc20   CIP

97 98 99 00 01 02 03 04 05 — 10 9 8 7 6 5 4 3 2

MANUFACTURED IN THE UNITED STATES OF AMERICA

Contents

A C K N O W L E D G M E N T S

This work is the result of creativity, encouragement, and the unselfishness of the fifteen contributors whose efforts made a desire a reality.

Special thanks to Vanessa Colston, Ralph Wheeler, Mary Simmons (Mom), Gardner Taylor, and Jana Childers for their untiring labor in making this a coherent, unified book. My gratitude to Ella Pearson Mitchell and the Mitchell family for their support.

Books

1970.   Black Preaching. Philadelphia and New York: J. B. Lippincott. Reprint, New York: Harper & Row, 1979.

1975.   *Black Belief: Folk Beliefs of Blacks in America and West Africa.* New York: Harper & Row.

1977.   *The Recovery of Preaching.* San Francisco: Harper & Row.

1986.   *Soul Theology: The Heart of American Black Culture.* Nicholas C. Cooper-Lewter, coauthor. San Francisco: Harper & Row. Paperback edition, Nashville: Abingdon Press, 1991.

1990.   *Black Preaching: The Recovery of a Powerful Art.* Nashville: Abingdon Press.

1990.   Celebration and Experience in Preaching. Nashville: Abingdon Press.

1993.   *A Study Guide to Accompany Celebration and Experience in Preaching.* Martha Simmons, coauthor. Self-published.

1994.   *Preaching for Black Self-Esteem.* Emile M. Thomas, coauthor. Nashville: Abingdon Press.

Articles and Chapters in Books Edited by Others

1972.   "Black English." In *Bridges.* Edited by Hazel G. Mobley and Elliot Roberts. Englewood Cliffs, N.J.: Prentice-Hall.

1976.   "A Drink of Water from Home: The Ministry of Identity." In *Preaching the Gospel.* Edited by Henry J. Young. Philadelphia: Fortress Press.

1983.   "The Justice of God." In *Biblical Preaching: An Expositor's Treasury.* Edited by James W. Cox. Philadelphia: Westminster Press, 1983.

1986.   "Black Preaching." In *Black Church Life-Styles,* edited by Emmanuel L. McCall. Nashville: Broadman Press.

1989.   "Toward a Theology of Black Preaching." In *African American Religious Studies: An Interdisciplinary Anthology.* Edited by Gayraud S. Wilmore. Durham, N.C.: Duke University Press.

1993.   "The Hearer's Experience of the Word." In *Listening to the Word: Studies in Honor of Fred B. Craddock.* Edited by Gail R. O'Day and Thomas Long. Nashville: Abingdon Press.

Articles and Essays in Journals and Periodicals

1966.   "Negro Worship and Universal Need." *The Christian Century* 83, no. 16 (March 30).

1967.   "Compensatory: Key Term in Theological Education of the Negro." *The Christian Century* 84, no. 17 (April 26). (Title was not the choice of the author.)

1968.   "Black Power and the Christian Church." In *Foundations: A Baptist Journal of History and Theology* 11, no. 2 (April–June).

1969.   "Reparations Without Repentance." *The Tower: Alumni Magazine of Union Theological Seminary* 16, no. 1 (fall).

1970.   "A Tale of Two Cities," Eddie S. O'Neil, coauthor. *The Christian Century* 88, no. 5 (February 3).

1970.   "Black Christianity in the Post Christian Era, U.S.A." *Black Scholar* (December).

1972.   "Celebration of a Stolen Gospel." *Home Missions* 43, no. 4 (April).

1973.   "Black Improvisation! Real and Imitation." *Freeing the Spirit* 2, no. 4.

1973.   "Black Preaching." *Review and Expositor: A Baptist Theological Journal* 70, no. 3 (summer)

1975.   "Some Preliminary Reflections on Authority in Black Religion." *Journal of the Interdenominational Theological Center* 3, no. 1.

1985.   "A Brief on Black Worship: Culture and Theology." *American Baptist Quarterly* 5, no. 4 (December).

1988.   "On Preaching to the Whole Person." *Pulpit Digest* 68 (January/February and March/April).

1989.   "To Suffer Long." *Pulpit Digest* 69, no. 499 (September/October).

1989.   "A Man After God's Own Heart." *Pulpit Digest* 69, no. 500 (November/December).

1991.   "The Awesome Meek." *Pulpit Digest* 72, no. 507 (January/February).

1992.   "Catching Hope." *The Living Pulpit* 1, no. 1 (January–March).

1992.   "Help for Unbelief." *The Living Pulpit* 1, no. 1 (April–June).

1993.   "Sometimes It Causes Me to Tremble." *The Living Pulpit* 2, no. 1 (January–March).

One cannot help noting that a book honoring the epic contributions of Henry Mitchell to the whole American religious experience is apt and long past due. What Dr. Mitchell has done for preachers and hearers of preachers in America is monumental.

Dr. Mitchell supplied American Christendom with an understanding of the importance, nature, and nuances of Black preaching. Before Mitchell's writings, for the majority of American Christendom, Black preaching was a "lost chord." Glorious has been the history of the pulpit in this country. It has claimed mighty voices, people mighty in the Spirit. Churchgoers have gazed upon preachers whose faces were made luminous by the fire of the gospel. Others have heard extraordinary preachers, pouring forth a torrent of eloquence. The church has known its seers with a sense of the higher altitudes of life and faith. Some have possessed voices that stir the old, forgotten dreams of the soul, touched by the demanding, beckoning temptations upward of that "still, small voice," which, though still and small, pounds in the soul like a thousand Niagras. Still something was missing.

Henry Mitchell introduced to America the "lost chord" of its preaching. The note America needed was of a preaching which, at its best, merged two worlds, the one that is and the one that is to be. The Black preacher was faced with a fearful task of theodicy—interpreting difficulties that made one feel that nobody could know the troubles one's soul had seen. It would take God to make such a person cry, *"Glory Hallelujah."* The Black preacher had to make known to a people bound in chains the glad tidings of liberation, when none was in sight, not even dimly. In a dark and seemingly endless night, Black preachers, often with cryptic phrases and a strange, solemn, eerie music in their voice, spoke of a morning soon to come. There was no evidence other than what God had said and done in the old record of the Bible, supremely in Jesus of Nazareth. With that record, one's faith, a language—sometimes almost unbearably poignant—and nothing else,

11

the Black preacher kept a sorely oppressed people on their feet, "facing the surely rising sun."

Dr. Mitchell's love for the sound and substance of what we know as Black preaching enabled him to present to the entire American religious undertaking the genius of the sable figure who stood, as the fathers said, "in the shoes of John," crying, "Behold. . . . "

As long as the gospel is uttered in our land, what Henry Mitchell has done in this regard must shine forth as a crucial gift to the work of God and to the worship of God's Son on these shores. The distinguished coterie of authors herein attests bountifully to the importance of his contributions and to how we can use and build upon these contributions as we all await a new century.

As Dr. Mitchell comes toward the sunset, with his ever lengthening shadow more and more behind him and with the cool of evening beginning to be felt, all of us who are beneficiaries of his works prayerfully hope that he may recognize, as we do, that he "came to the Kingdom for such a time as this."

Gardner Taylor
Brooklyn, New York
June 1995

The title of this book, Preaching on the Brink, *was* selected to emphasize Henry Mitchell's concern that the study of preaching have a positive impact on the myriad societal issues that await us on the cusp of a new century and a new millennium.

The fifteen essays in this book resonate with the tone and tenor of Henry H. Mitchell's work. Beginning with his unparalleled work *Black Preaching*, Mitchell's early work addressed the issues of helping preachers to *sit where their listeners sit* (existentially and culturally) and the absolute prerequisite that preaching speak to persons holistically (emotively, intuitively, and cognitively). His work of the last decade has finely focused on the need for preaching that is *behaviorally targeted* and most often *celebrative in outcome*. His works can be categorized with four emphases: (1) audience identification; (2) the form and content of preaching; (3) praxis; and (4) the personality (personal involvement) of the preacher.

These essays will not simply regurgitate, analyze, or enshrine the life and writings of Henry Mitchell. Instead, they are intended by his colleagues and friends to continue Mitchell's tradition of offering material that is useful for the academy and for the practitioner.

Part One: Upon Whose Ears? addresses the presence of a type of listener and how that impacts the substance of preaching and our approach toward proclamation. It begins with Barbara Brown Zikmund's appraisal of the current battles of women in ministry. Susan D. Newman encounters baby boomers and defines the tools required when preaching to distinct groups of boomers. Robert M. Franklin concludes this section with an essay focusing on one of the most notably absent groups in the American church, African American men.

Part Two: What Is Being Heard? concerns the substance and character of preaching. Eugene L. Lowry addresses how preachers can functionally preach great themes and discusses the attending impact of such preaching. Fred B. Craddock asks that we revisit the use of rhetoric and urges that we not hastily forget its historical value to preaching nor how it can still benefit preaching. David Buttrick writes to homileticians and indirectly speaks to students, proposing an umbrella curriculum for teaching preaching for a new century. Paul Scott Wilson questions our use of doctrines in preaching and explores whether they have a role in future approaches to sermon preparation and proclamation. James Earl Massey lifts up sage prerequisites for preachers who want to be perceived and received as teachers.

Part Three: Into All the World concerns itself with where listeners are encountered and how sermons can resound beyond church walls and Sunday mornings. J. Alfred Smith Sr. says the city has been dramatically altered and focuses on what it means to preach in this context. Richard Ward analyzes the impact of television on gospel proclamation. Barbara Harris designs a "movement model" for twenty-first-century preaching, for vast numbers of churches located in cities that are unclean, indigent, dilapidated, and dispirited.

Part Four: How Shall We Preach? concludes the festschrift. Contributors grapple with how the preaching moment is affected by imagination, gender, prophetic stance, and a minister's personal ethics. Thomas H. Troeger lifts up modernistic tools to enhance the use of imagination in preaching. Edwina Hunter declares that women should be different types of proclaimers than men. Samuel D. Proctor describes the twenty-first-century prophet twenty-five years after the death of Martin Luther King Jr. Last but not least, William H. Willimon thoughtfully attends the subject of the preacher's personal ethics and their import for the preaching moment.

Dedicated to Dr. Henry H. Mitchell

G R A T I T U D E

They were there like lampposts when you were lost,
shading and shining light in those crevices
that no one else regarded.

They helped you grasp varied, quicksilver realities.
But more salvific, more etched in your soul, is their
contagious belief in you that procured the transport
for your life's adventure.

But were you in step with the ninety and nine
who went on their way
or the one who went back?

But what about that disrobing of your apprehensions,
and the lessons that led to the conversion and the visions
that propelled you. And once you made your mark,
it fell on you, like a millstone around your neck;
they impacted your sojourn and never sought remuneration.

But were you in step with the ninety and nine
who went on their way
or the one who went back?

To all teachers unacclaimed, all mentors unrequited,
alive or transitioned, please accept our deficient language,
as we only have words,
to proclaim what we must say.

We are many, and we do now testify, testify, testify!

O N   T H E
M A K I N G   O F   A
H O M I L E T I C I A N

*H*enry Herbert Mitchell Sr. grew up in a three-bedroom house in Columbus, Ohio. During his childhood and early teens, Mitchell viewed himself as a midget. He was quite short, less than five feet tall and scrawny. He weighed about ninety pounds. He was tormented by the fact that he did not clearly appear to be African American. His skin color resembled that of a slightly tanned white male. His hair was jet black and straight, and his eyes were slanted as if indicating Asian ancestry. To add to the lack of self-esteem that he secretly felt because he was scrawny and thin, children often made fun of his physical features, which they found easy targets for horrible epithets, such as "Ching chong, Chinaman, eats dead rats, chews them up like ginger snaps."

Such treatment made Mitchell an inhibited child who worked hard to be more of an impressive presence. Taking care of his ailing mother, cooking, and doing housework allowed him to develop an early maturity and a toughness that could at least help shield him from the torturous darts thrown by children unaware. In developing this maturity he also quickly learned how to type, play a violin, hang a door, lay a floor, install plumbing, and build a house. Today we would call him a Renaissance man.

Mitchell was one of four siblings, with his two brothers, Elbert and Lewis, and his sister, Marjorie. He was reared by Christian parents who introduced the children to God before the children could speak. There is not a time when Mitchell can recall not believing in God or the need to be led by the Word of God. The call of God was already an issue for him by age six. He had been named after two grandfathers (Henry Estes and Henry Mitchell), both of whom were Baptist preachers. However, he was not impressed by what either of his grandfathers had to show for all of their high integrity and solid work in ministry. By the time he was ten, both men were living on old-age assistance. Both of Mitchell's parents, who were committed to the work of the church, had bitter memories of how their fathers had been ill-treated and even victimized by congregations. This was enough to make Mitchell resolve that he would never preach.

By age fourteen, Mitchell *knew* what God wanted him to do, but he continued to ask God to show it to him more plainly. The presence of God in his life was daily made clear by his father, who used any opportunity to quote scriptures and show their applicability to all of life. Early on, this gave Mitchell a sense that God was present in every aspect of his life, providentially guiding him. Just as Mitchell was about to surrender to God's call, there was a great controversy in the church he attended over a minister who had been instrumental in using youth in prayer meetings, starting scout troops and the like. This seventy-year-old preacher was Mitchell's hero, and Mitchell was convinced that he was viciously, wrongfully accused. But like Mitchell's grandfathers, rather than fight it out, the old minister retired. The old patterns of mistreatment that his grandfathers had endured had emerged again, so he stopped praying the prayer about finding God's will for his life. In fact, he almost stopped praying altogether.

Wrassling Up a Future

In 1937, at age seventeen, Mitchell finished high school. He began giving thought to "wrassling up a future" for himself. He went to work in his home church as a social worker for flood refugees. Following this brief stint, Mitchell got a better job, paying twenty-five cents an hour. This was quite a bit of money for a seventeen-year-old Negro boy during the Depression. While on this job, Mitchell often sat alone installing spade lugs on tractor wheels, and during these solitary times the matter of life vocation reared its head again. He evaded it again and again, but it would not leave. It often followed him to bed and encountered him in his dreams. Finally Mitchell yielded to the call to preach. He told his mother, a church social worker, and she expressed no surprise. She told him that she had prayed that the Lord would call him. She had often spoken to his brother about being called to preach, but never to him. "Somehow I just knew it would happen," she said.

In 1939 Mitchell found himself away from home at college. A year at Ohio State and then three at Lincoln University were full of new experiences and years during which he often found himself short on funds and edibles, but his past lessons had buttressed him with survival skills. Most of all, he knew he could depend on the God in whom he had grown up delighting. He worked as a waiter, a teaching assistant in English, an elevator operator, a mechanic's helper, a janitor, warehouseman, and a lifeguard. He graduated from Lincoln with a Bachelor's degree in English.

After graduation, a desire to study for the professional ministry took him to Union Theological Seminary in New York City. There, his belief in the need for holistic ministry was shaped by his fieldwork in Harlem and by professors such as Reinhold Niebuhr, Paul Tillich, Harry Emerson Fosdick, Ralph Sockman, and George Buttrick. These theological and homiletical legends heightened Mitchell's love of ministry, preaching, and scholarship. While he marveled at the knowledge these men possessed, he knew that something was missing from their instruction and their analysis of the Bible, homiletics, and theology. That something was an understanding of his culture. Mitchell knew that someone had to write about the religious contributions and methodologies of his people for use in seminaries. Only this would enable Black students to receive the type of educational experience needed to do ministry within their own communities. While in seminary, he gained invaluable pastoral experience working as an assistant to the pastor of Concord Baptist Church in Brooklyn, New York.

At Union, Mitchell developed severe appendicitis and pneumonia. As he lay shrouded by death, lingering in a hospital without modern wonder drugs such as penicillin and sulfur, the doctors assembled and concluded that his illness would be fatal. At this point, his father, who had a terrible fear of flying, took an airplane to New York to be at his son's bedside. During his vigil, Mitchell's father took his meals at the seminary cafeteria. Often, he sat in the cafeteria and wept. Most students, who were praying for his son's health, may not have noticed his tears, but Ella Pearson did, and she spent time consoling him. After several weeks, Mitchell's health began to improve. As Mitchell's foreparents would say, "God spared him and allowed his golden moments to roll on a little while longer."

After a broken engagement, which Mitchell later called a providential blessing, Mitchell told his father about his concern that he couldn't find a wife. His father replied, "What about that Pearson girl?" Mitchell responded, "Well, Dad, she's not quite what I had in mind. She's bigger than me and she's older." But as he did for all major decisions, he called on the God who had always shown him the way. After praying for hours one morning, the Lord said to Mitchell the same thing that his father had said. Because of his unfounded reputation that he was a slick-haired playboy, it took some doing for Mitchell to win Ella Pearson's affection, but in 1944 they married. After graduation from Union, he went on to become the acting dean of chapel, director of religious activities, and an English instructor at what was then North Carolina School for Negroes.

Building a Family and a Career

Although there were some who wondered about Mitchell's race, it did not keep him from knowing the sting of racial oppression any less than any other Negro. In the 1940s, while on a train ride with students and his wife, Mitchell was asked to move from a train car because it contained White passengers. Since the area of the train reserved for Negros was quite full and there was a partition separating Negro passengers from White passengers, and since there were very few White passengers, Mitchell refused to move. The porter left and returned with a sheriff who waved a large gun in Mitchell's face and said, "Move!" At that moment, Mitchell says, "I decided, as I looked at my wife who was pregnant with our first child, I'll see this child in heaven first, before I'll move from this seat." The men, apparently stunned by Mitchell's unflinching courage, backed down. This type of quiet, courageous activism marked Mitchell's life and involved him in the Civil Rights movement.

The next decade of Mitchell's life included his first experience with parenthood and a deepening of his experience in ministry. After the birth of his first child, Henry Mitchell Jr., Mitchell became a work-horse, holding joint appointments with the General Baptist Association of Northern California, the Northern California Baptist Convention, and the American Baptist Churches Home Mission Society. His territory of oversight stretched from Bakersfield, California, to the Oregon border. His varied gifts and skills (proposal writer, Spanish interpreter, administrator, and teacher) allowed him during these joint appointments to be a resource person for more than eighty-five churches from 1945 to 1959. Most of the churches he served were African American, but Mitchell also helped organize several White churches. During these years he also found time to serve as the director of the educational center operated by what is now the Northern California American Baptist Churches of the West. In this position he provided in-service training for pastors, pastoral placement, arbitration services for churches, assistance in court for churches, Christian education and lay leadership institutes, and directed bilingual work. He was also editor of their monthly magazine, *The Baptist Advance*, and the assistant to the executive secretary of the organization. The Goliath-like nature of Mitchell's energy and skills was underscored when it took four people, three full-time and one part-time, to replace him after he accepted the call of Second Baptist Church in Fresno, California. It was his first full-time pastorate.

With the birth of two daughters, Muriel and Elizabeth, Mitchell was pleased to have more time to spend with his family. He found the pastorate fulfilling. He greatly enjoyed ministering to people and preaching each Sunday. He was also exhilarated by the church's work to uplift the community.

In 1949, Mitchell's only sister, the baby of the family, was brutally murdered at age twenty-one. Mitchell says that during the trial of the killer, for the first and only time in his life, he wanted to take the life of another—either the killer or his lawyer, or both. The killer was ultimately released on a legal technicality. After the trial, Mitchell knew that he had to forgive his sister's killer. During this ordeal he learned that if he continued to harbor such deep hatred, he would be immobilized and would spread his anger to his family and friends. Again he leaned, this time hard, on the God to whom he had given control of his life. God helped him to do what he could not do on his own, forgive the killer of someone he loved.

Several years later, the Mitchells adopted a boy, whom they named Ken. Ken had been left in a field in Korea to die. No one knew the child's actual age; he was presumed to be about four and a half years old when he joined the Mitchell family. The social worker showed them pictures of Ken and expressed, "I know you don't want such a dark child." Mitchell asked, "Is he healthy? Can he talk?" The social worker replied, "Oh yes, oh yes, but he's quite rebellious." "Then that's our boy," said Mitchell. "He needs to be a bit rebellious, given what he's gone through," and the adoption was completed.

While pastoring the church in Fresno, Mitchell's serious interest in homiletics sprouted. During this period he studied linguistics and received a master's degree from Fresno State College. After six years he concluded his first pastorate. Although he accomplished a great deal in Fresno, he left unsatisfied that he hadn't done more. While he would never call his first stint in the pastorate a failure, he will now admit that some in the church felt that he moved too fast for them. However, in later years members from this church also commented to him about how much he was missed and how much good he had done.

Mitchell was called to pastor another church less than six months after leaving his first. This was a pastorate filled with lawsuits. At times Mitchell led worship on the church steps. There were constant skirmishes between trustees, deacons, and members. Mitchell pastored only a year and a half in peace at this church. Subsequently, he served as the interim pastor for three other churches.

By this time, Mitchell had begun devoting more attention to academics and writing. By 1969, he was steeped in the study of African and African American culture and had already published more than twenty articles and a textbook titled *How Churches Teach*. Now he was known across the country in denominational conventions and church education venues because of the work done during his joint appointments from 1945 to 1959. After leaving the pastorate, Mitchell longed to go back. However, he also knew that God had always guided his life and had never made a mistake. With this assurance, he went where he now knows that God intended him to be all along, to the world of academia.

The Dean Arrives

Mitchell's notoriety for working with preachers and for his studies in African American worship and culture caused him to be hired in 1969 as the Martin Luther King Jr. Professor of Black Church Studies at Colgate Rochester Divinity School. This position, unlike any before it, established Mitchell's teaching career. It occasioned the second of eight trips to Africa to research his religious and cultural heritage. It was also with this position that Mitchell laid the foundation for his being dubbed "The Dean of Teachers of Black Preachers." At Colgate Rochester, with the King Fellows, Mitchell brought together a class of Black preachers and educators unmatched before or since. The group included John Bryant, now a bishop in The African Methodist Episcopal Church; Dr. Harold Carter, pastor and author of several books, most recently *The Myths That Mire the Ministry*; Phillip Cousins, now a bishop in the A.M.E. Church; James Forbes Jr., a professor at Union Seminary and pastor of Riverside Church; William Augustus Jones, former president of the Progressive Baptist Convention and pastor of the three-thousand-member Bethany Baptist Church; Wyatt Walker; Dr. Elliott Mason; H. Beecher Hicks Jr.; and eleven others. Mitchell was assisted with this first-of-its-kind program by professors Thelma Adair, M. Franchesca Thompson, and Ella Pearson Mitchell.

In 1970, at age fifty, Mitchell's seminal work *Black Preaching* was published. Just as Mitchell was gaining a solid footing as an academician, his son Henry Jr. died of leukemia following radiation exposure. Shortly afterward, Mitchell was the target of a painful attack by several African American master of divinity students at Colgate. They refused to take a test that was to be administered by Mitchell and threatened the dean with a boycott. The students claimed that the test lacked relevance and that Mitchell had already administered too many exams during the semester. Students such as these were the very people whom Mitchell had longed to teach and to introduce to their foreparent's rich contributions to religion. Following these two painful episodes in his life, Mitchell lingered in bed, convinced that he was dying of an unknown cause. He was later diagnosed as severely depressed. Eventually, he took a leave of absence from Colgate Rochester and returned to California.

Remarkably, even during this period his creativity remained intractable and he never wearied of work. His passion for homiletics and his conviction that this was his calling kept him going. After returning to California, he served as a visiting professor and earned his Doctor of Theology degree from Claremont School of Theology in less than a year. In 1974 he delivered the prestigious Lyman Beecher Lectures at Yale. They were subsequently expanded and published as *The Recovery of Preaching.*

By 1975, Mitchell, already well established as an authority on Black preaching and Black church education, published *Black Belief.* It represented the culmination of years of study in Africa and of Black life in America. Mitchell presented the manuscript before the Society for the Study of Black Religion. Unfortunately, unlike the warm response he had received when *Black Preaching* was published, the Society's critique of his work was scathing. For many years, Mitchell was scarred by this frosty reception by his peers. The fact is, Mitchell's homiletical skills were always ahead of his time.

In fact, his skills as a academician were so considerable that they overshadowed his preaching skills. Mitchell, along with few others, brought to the Black church an approach to preaching that contained not only emotion, but also critical exegesis and the latest in theological concepts. But his approach did not contain a "tune," the hallmark of Black preaching prized by most of the Black church community.

Although he has trained more Black clergy than any of the major homileticians of the twentieth century, Mitchell has been more celebrated by White clergy and homileticians than by his Black colleagues. Still, his love of Black culture and Black preaching, which he considered an art form that had to be written about in order to enrich homiletics, helped him to persevere. Additionally, he felt a special commitment to working with Black students and Black preachers who rarely saw academicians who looked like them or understood their culture.

Through major personal and professional disappointments, Mitchell held on to his belief in his calling. He allowed God to use him to broaden the study of preaching. He used adversity instead of allowing adversity to control him. The passion in his writings and classroom instruction is born of Mitchell's immovable belief in the providence of God, and in his favorite scripture: "All things work together for good for those who love God and are called according to God's purposes" (Rom. 8:28, Mitchell's paraphrase).

For the Academy and All

Henry Mitchell's legacy of writings, lectures, and classroom instruction represents a major contribution to the church universal. By the late seventies the White academies of preaching had begun to realize that Henry Mitchell was an important contributor to the field, as they had not previously seen. His writings contained elements that have always been the sine qua non of academic distinction. His work also made clear what few in the academy had been wise enough to realize— that Black preaching is a sanctified art form containing principles useful for the church universal.

For years, Mitchell admits, he scrupulously avoided using the writings of Whites in his books and articles. He had seen enough of them as a student. Further, he was convinced that all that he needed to say about preaching could be said by him, his foreparents, and his community. In later years, during a period of what he called "looking back growth," Mitchell determined that his work would not be compromised by dialogue with White theologians and homileticians. By the time of his writing of *Celebration and Experience in Preaching*, he was able to proclaim what he knew all along, that the good news about good preaching was a story that could be claimed by all and shared with all.

From 1982 to 1986, Mitchell served as the dean for Virginia Union Seminary. From 1988 to 1995 he team-taught homiletics with his wife at the Interdenominational Theological Center in Atlanta. During this period Mitchell endured a number of surgeries. One resulted in some loss of vision and another involved a difficult course of chemotherapy. Two angioplasties meant an extended period of recovery. Out of it all came what may be his finest sermon to date, "No More Bad Days."

In 1989 he began teaching in the doctor of ministry program at United Theological Seminary in Dayton, Ohio. Over the last seven years, Mitchell, concerned with passing on a legacy in light of the challenges ahead for the church, has begun writing with other preachers and homileticians. Such works have included *Soul Theology*, written with Nicholas C. Cooper-Lewter, *A Workbook to Accompany Celebration and Experience in Preaching*, written with this editor, and *Preaching for Black Self-Esteem*, written with Emil M. Thomas.

In the mid-eighties Mitchell moved to Atlanta to be closer to some of his children and to spend more time with his six grandchildren. At this writing, Mitchell is seventy-six, an active family barber, beginning work on a joint autobiography with his wife of fifty-one years, teaching at United Seminary, and mentoring his youngest daughter through the completion of her master of divinity degree. As a future project, he plans to write a book on the history of the African American church in America.

Mitchell's texts have been used in seminaries for a quarter century, and discussions about his contributions have been numerous. Although the totality of what Mitchell has given to homiletics and the study of Black culture may never be known, there are four indisputable contributions:

First, *Mitchell, more than anyone in this century, has legitimated Black preaching as an important art form in America*, the genius of which has positive implications for all preaching.

Second, *he is the architect of the use of a behavioral purpose in sermons* (giving attention to who hearers are as total beings and to what they *do* after hearing a sermon).

Third, *he was the first to advocate the need to conclude almost every sermon with a celebration* (concluding with good news).

Finally, *he has worked untiringly to simply get preachers to see that during the preaching moment, hearers need a picture or a story with which they can identify.*

As the twenty-first century looms large before the church, replete with marvelous opportunities and disheartening realities, we take comfort in the homiletical legacy that Henry H. Mitchell Sr. has given to us. What we do with the legacy shall, in large measure, determine our response when we are asked, "In times like these, what is the word from the Lord, and how shall we hear it without a preacher?"

PART ONE

UPON WHOSE EARS?

CHAPTER ONE

Barbara Brown Zikmund

WHAT OF ALL THESE WOMEN IN THE CHURCH?

Henry Mitchell, as spouse of a clergywoman for fifty years, father of a clergywoman, and mentor to countless clergywomen, knows firsthand about a subject that has caused more pain (but offers more potential for renewal) than any issue the church could address, save perhaps the church honestly wrestling with racism. That subject is the equitable treatment of women by the church.

When we want to celebrate the inclusive message of the Christian gospel, it is quite common for preachers to quote Paul's Letter to the Galatians, "There is no longer Jew or Greek, there is no longer slave or free, there is no longer male and female; for all of you are one in Christ Jesus" (Gal. 3:28 NRSV).

In reality, however, the history of the Christian church is filled with inequities. There have been doctrinal and racial divisions, there have been cultural and economic groupings, and there have been pervasive gender assumptions that have kept the church "out of balance." We may be one in Christ Jesus, but in the church we live with perverse lopsidedness. Historical theology, religious sociology, and ethical commentary witness to the ways in which the ideal of Christian unity contrasts with reality.

Relationships between women and men in the church are a good illustration. Over the centuries, the leadership of the church has been male-dominated, while membership has been overwhelmingly female. As far as I can tell, this pattern developed in the early and medieval church, was recast in new forms in the sixteenth-century Reformation, and persists into the modern era. Only within the past 150 years have women and men begun to challenge long-standing gender assumptions about leadership and membership in the church—asking, "What of all these women in the church?"

Contemporary historian Gerda Lerner suggests that our new awareness of gender is having dramatic consequences. In fact, the contemporary feminist movement has a significance equal to that of the Copernican Revolution, because it exposes the error of all androcentric or patriarchal thought patterns and practices. As we come to recognize that human experience is always "gendered," we are undergoing a revolution in human comprehension fully as dramatic as learning to see the sun at the center of the planetary system.[1]

This revolution in human comprehension about the relationships between women and men and their roles in society is found in several movements. First there is the *women's movement*. The women's movement is that broad-based historical movement wherein women in western Europe and North America in the nineteenth and twentieth centuries challenged dominant governments and social theories in order to gain increased political and social freedom.

Second, there is the specific drive for *women's emancipation*, especially in public life. Women and men within the women's movement focus upon achieving political and legal equality by gaining the vote for women. In America, the first wave of the women's movement culminated in 1920 with the ratification of the nineteenth amendment to the United States Constitution, giving women the right to vote.

Supporters of women's suffrage had diverse motivations: some felt that the vote would ensure equal rights for women; others felt that the vote would enable women to protect their special responsibilities within the home and family.

Third, there is the modern *women's liberation movement*, or *feminism*. Women's liberation and feminism usually refer to a "second wave" of activity beginning in the 1960s, whereby women actively seek, as Roman Catholic theologian Sandra Schneiders writes, "liberation *from* marginalization, oppression, discrimination, and violence [and] freedom *for* self-definition, self-affirmation, and self-determination....The contemporary [women's liberation] movement envisions not only political and legal rights for women equal to those of men, but the liberation of women (and men) into the fullness of human personhood." Such liberation requires more than the reform of current arrangements; it calls for "a total transformation of ideology and structures, a reimagining of personal and social reality that will leave no person, group, or institution unchanged."[2]

For some people, however, this is too much. In the 1990s there is a fourth development. Women and men are reacting against feminism and retreating back to earlier attitudes and expectations. They are troubled by what has happened. As one young woman writes, "In dispensing its spoils, women's liberation has given my generation high incomes, our own cigarette, the option of single parenthood, rape crisis centers, personal lines of credit, free love, and female gynecologists. . . . In return it has effectively robbed us of one thing upon which the happiness of most women rests—men."[3] As Susan Faludi has noted, since the 1980s it has been increasingly popular to "hold the campaign for women's equality responsible for nearly every woe besetting women."[4]

Although such a reversal is overstated, it is true that younger women are challenging earlier feminist assumptions. Rene Denfeld reports, in a new book entitled *The New Victorians: A Young Woman's Challenge to the Old Feminist Order*, that she is impatient with "her radical foremothers" and appalled by extremists who neglect real-life issues in favor of bashing men, worshiping the Goddesses, battling porn-mongers, and denouncing heterosexuality. But, she insists, it is this stridency and intolerance, not a sexist backlash, that has driven young women away from the movement. She is worried that a vocal minority exhibiting a new Victorian-style "moral and spiritual" crusade against feminist extremists will ultimately destroy women's sexual freedom and undermine their political clout. Denfeld and others insist that the modern women's movement must press for balanced political reform and social change that will put women on an equal footing with men in all settings.[5]

Women in the Black church dramatically illustrate the ups and downs of these changing attitudes about gender. In the Black church women are rarely "on the pulpit." This is because the pulpit has been viewed as "men's space" and the pew as "women's place." C. Eric Lincoln and Lawrence H. Mamiya, in *The Black Church in the African American Experience*, note that this understanding of the pulpit as men's space and the pew as women's place is found not only in Black churches, but also in most White churches. It draws upon the patriarchal view that the public sphere is male space and the private sphere is female space.[6] A similar sexual division of public and private matters also appears in Judaism and Islam.

How did this understanding of women's secondary place in the church evolve? Why have there continually been more women than men in the pews and fewer women than men exercising visible leadership in all areas of the Christian church? A partial answer can be found in American history.

Colonial America began with more gender balance than was found in many parts of the Western Hemisphere. The English Separatists and Puritans who immigrated to Massachusetts in the 1620s came to the New World to make permanent settlement. These men, women, and children left their homes and founded new communities and churches—understanding themselves to be on "an errand into the wilderness" in search of religious and economic well-being.

In these settings American Puritan women were crucial agents in cultivating household religiosity. Inasmuch as female piety served as the cornerstone for family religious life, women needed to be educated so that they could raise morally upright children. Their Christian discipleship, however, was not expected to contribute significantly to wider church life.

Gradually, the situation changed. By the early eighteenth century, female church membership increased and American women expanded their relationship to church and society. During the great revivals or awakenings in the 1730s and 1740s, American women were viewed positively. In 1725, the famous Puritan leader Cotton Mather called women "People who make no Noise at all in the World: People hardly Known to be in the world; but people who were nevertheless the salvation of the church." Cotton Mather noted that "as there were three Maries to one John standing under the Cross of our dying Lord, so still there are far more *godly Women,* than there are *godly Men.*"[7]

By the early nineteenth century, the ideals of female piety in American Protestantism had shifted from cultivating individual charity and devotion to active engagement through voluntary female organizations within and outside the churches. At the same time, understandings of clergy changed. "Church work" was done by laity, many of whom were women. Clergy (most of whom were male) taught and preached, and also identified themselves with emerging denominational religious structures. Furthermore, as churches were disestablished (removed from connection to the prevailing political order) clergy focused upon retaining power in the wider society.

With the dawn of the twentieth century, women's work in the church centered on three areas. First, women served in places where men could not function. This usually meant that women had special responsibilities for educational and medical ministries to women and children at home and abroad. Many intelligent and able American women went into the mission field as teachers and doctors, doing things in far distant places that they never would have been allowed to do at home. Thousands of supportive church women raised special money to support women's work. They organized independent women's mission boards to get the job done, and to have a more direct say in how it was done.

Second, women worked in places where men refused to work. In the ethnic ghettos of growing cities, women provided services to needy families. Protestant deaconesses and Christian settlement house workers inspired young women to serve the needy in society until they married and started their own families. Women were found in places where the rhetoric of charity needed to be maintained, but the men did not want to do the work—especially when they would have received little or no pay. Church work, volunteer and paid, became the primary expression of Christian women's faith. What a woman did as a Christian volunteer was a gift to her family, her church, and the wider society.

This understanding of women's role, often called the "cult of domesticity," assumed that women's place was in the home and the church; and within the church, she belonged in the classroom, the choir, and the kitchen. Women had a natural inclination toward religion and righteousness, and women were morally superior to men. Out of their moral purity and spiritual superiority women would save the home, the churches, the nation, and even the pagan world. As men abandoned religion in their struggle for political power and economic well-being, women were called to tend their families and their churches, and to exercise important influence behind the scenes. Through their moral virtue and religious fervor, women were the key to redemption.[8]

Today men and women in a variety of churches continue to operate under the cult of domesticity. Women outnumber the men in the pews, in the church school, and behind the scenes, while the majority of clergy remain male. It is true that during the past thirty years the number of women in seminaries has dramatically increased, and many denominations have relaxed their rules against the ordination of women. In spite of these developments, the ecclesiastical climate is still very chilly for many women who want to do more than follow traditional patterns shaped by the cult of domesticity. Women can be "paid volunteers" or "the laity who do the ministry," but men lead the way. *Pervasive habits of membership roles and leadership roles continue to hold the church of Jesus Christ hostage.*

In the face of this situation, contemporary preaching cannot remain silent. It must become proactive. Remember how the angel of the Lord appeared to Philip and called him to go down to the wilderness road from Jerusalem to Gaza. When he got there, Philip overheard a eunuch from the royal court of Ethiopia, sitting in his chariot and reading from the prophet Isaiah. And the Spirit said to Philip, "Go over to this chariot and join it." So Philip went and he asked the man, "Do you understand what you are reading?" To which the man replied, "How can I, unless someone guides me?" Philip got into the chariot and convinced the man that the Scriptures had been fulfilled in Jesus Christ. Eventually the eunuch asked to be baptized, and his life was changed (Acts 8:26-40 NRSV).

This is what is needed. Women are traveling that wilderness road from Jerusalem to Gaza, that road from their supportive "behind the scenes" roles to more public and creative opportunities for service in the church, that road from the work that no one else will do in church and society, to additional work that God wants done to change our world. Women are on that road that leads from the pew to the pulpit, and those who are presently in the pulpits need to do more than watch from afar.

Part of the conversation on the road is remembering the legacies of women that fall outside the cult of domesticity. Within the Black church there is a wonderful heritage of female religious leadership. There were powerful oral traditions of Black Americans, kept most splendidly, often, by women. And there is that Spirit-led understanding within all of Protestantism that the call to preach and minister to one's people is ultimately legitimatized by deep personal experience that cannot be denied.[9] Such undeniable personal experience was exemplified by the Quakers in seventeenth-century America. Several of the early voices for women's rights, as well as those speaking out against slavery, would be Quaker women ministers, including Lucretia Mott.[10]

I believe that the Spirit is calling all of us who are already preaching to do as Philip did—to go over to those women (that chariot) and to join it. We need to travel that road with our sisters, of all races, prodding them to see their ministries beyond traditional roles. *We dare not let past habits of pew and pulpit distort the gospel.*

Every preacher, male and female, should be encouraging women on their journey, should be sharing the gospel of Jesus Christ to empower women who feel the call to preach. Many contemporary women will not ask us to guide them, for they follow an inner compass; but we need to support them.

Preachers create a climate in their congregations that enables young men and women to explore God's claim on their lives. This is especially true during the preaching moment. In the past, the cult of domesticity has limited the horizons of women. Efforts, even those that were well-intended, to support male clergy and to strengthen the public voice of the church in a patriarchal and secular society, have kept women from hearing the Word of God. Girls and women have been personally frustrated and kept down by internal attitudes and external rules, and the entire church has suffered.

What of all these women in the church today? They are an untapped resource for the renewal of the church. They are already in the churches, praying, teaching, singing, and serving. *Preachers have a responsibility to nourish a new climate for these women that will release new energy that has been thwarted for centuries.* With the prophet Joel, we dare not forget that God has promised, "Then afterward I will pour out my spirit on all flesh; your sons and your daughters shall prophesy, your old men shall dream dreams, and your young men shall see visions" (Joel 2:28 NRSV). May it be according to God's Word.

N O T E S

1. Gerda Lerner, *The Creation of Patriarchy* (New York: Oxford University Press, 1986), p. 13.
2. Sandra M. Schneiders, *Beyond Patching: Faith and Feminism in the Catholic Church* (Mahwah, N.J.: Paulist Press, 1991), p. 8.
3. Mona Charen, "The Feminist Mistake," *National Review* (23 March 1984), p. 24, quoted in Susan Faludi, *Backlash: The Undeclared War Against American Women* (New York: Doubleday, 1991), p. x.
4. Susan Faludi, *Backlash: The Undeclared War Against American Women* (New York: Doubleday, 1991), p. xi.
5. Rene Denfeld, *The New Victorians: A Young Woman's Challenge to the Old Feminist Order* (New York: Warner Books, 1995).
6. C. Eric Lincoln and Lawrence H. Mamiya, *The Black Church in the African American Experience* (Durham, N.C.: Duke University Press, 1990), p. 274, p. 451 n. 1.
7. Cotton Mather, *El-Shaddi. A Brief Essay . . . Produced by the Death of . . . Mrs. Katharine Williard.* Boston, 1725, quoted in Gerald F. Moran, "'The Hidden Ones:' Women and Religion in Puritan New England," in *Triumph over Silence: Women in Protestant History,* ed. Richard L. Greaves (Westport, Conn.: Greenwood Press, 1985), p. 21.
8. Barbara MacHaffie, *Herstory: Women in Christian Tradition* (Philadelphia: Fortress Press, 1986), p. 94.
9. C. Eric Lincoln and Lawrence H. Mamiya, *The Black Church*, pp. 277-78.
10. David Albert Farmer and Edwina Hunter, eds., *And Blessed Is She: Sermons by Women* (San Francisco: Harper & Row, 1990), pp. 6-7.

Susan D. Newman

P R E A C H I N G

T O   B A B Y

B O O M E R S

As the pastor of a predominantly African American church, I frequently focus on preaching to baby boomers. My perspective has implications for those preaching to congregations with dissimilar constituencies.

Our churches are filled with members of the most recent baby boom generation. These are the post–World War II babies. They are now between thirty and fifty. They are married, many for the second time. Many are single parents. They are career women and men. They have college degrees, vocational training, and little or no training. They are working and looking for work. They have homes in the suburbs, and in the inner city, rent high-rise luxury apartments, low-income apartments, and are homeless. They commute to work and work at home with computers and modems.

There are two distinct subgenerations within the baby boom generation. There is the thirty-five to forty-two age-group and the forty-three to fifty age-group. The thirty-five- to forty-two-year-old group was born between 1953 and 1960. They came of age during the Black Power movement. They were the ones who demanded rather than asked, argued rather than acquiesced. They believed in self-defense rather than turning the other cheek. And many of them considered religion the opiate of the masses. They respected the memory of Dr. Martin Luther King Jr., but did not identify with his program. These were the "children of promise." They had no counterpart to the Civil Rights movement. They remembered only Dr. King's funeral, not Dr. King. They did not have Malcolm X, but they did have his autobiography and Claude Brown's *Manchild in the Promised Land.*

As the "children of promise," they were the affirmative action babies. They were told that they would be equipped with the education and opportunity to advance in American society despite their race. They possessed a new view of integrated America. They were not awestruck with White people. They did not have stars in their eyes about integration. They realized that the African American businesses their parents grew up with no longer existed, and they believed that integration was largely responsible for the demise of these businesses. They were the generation that reached back to find their connection to Africa and who became active in organizations such as the African Liberation Support Committee. They participated in "line struggle" meetings over Mao's "Little Red Book." Unlike their grandparents, they were not concerned about "pie in the sky by and by"; rather they wanted "steak on my plate while I wait." This generation expects people to reach out and relate to them. They expect preachers to make the Bible relevant to their worldview.

The forty-three to fifty age-group was born between 1945 and 1952. They were teens and young adults during the Civil Rights movement. They were members of the Student Nonviolent Coordinating Committee (SNCC). They were members of the Southern Christian Leadership Conference (SCLC). They were the ones who bred integration.

One segment of this subgeneration was nonviolent and wanted to work with government to bring about changes in society. The other segment of the forty-three to fifty age-group consists of those who were members or supporters of the Black Panther party. The Black Panthers set up programs to feed the hungry and provided free medical clinics. They did not believe in conforming to the governmental structures in place to help African Americans. They developed strategies to answer societal ills without government intervention.

It is these two very challenging subgenerations of baby boomers that ministers must address at the "preaching moment." *Those who preach to baby boomers must raise, during sermon preparation, critical questions about life and about how one's faith interprets the answer to life's questions.* To do this, the preacher must lift up several possible sides of an issue and several viable solutions. These solutions must be anchored in the Word of God and must challenge the minds and the faith of the hearers.

Encounter Before Entering the Pulpit

Dr. Henry Mitchell, in his book *The Recovery of Preaching*, provides the key for preaching to today's boomers:

> First, one cannot generate a rerun of an experience one has never had nor personally appropriated. One's depths cannot cry out a message or conviction never lodged in those sacred precincts in the first place. To proclaim truth transconsciously one must possess it likewise, or at a gut level. . . . It is a waste of time to try to help a person build a sermon about anything that is not deeply his or hers. [1]

Mitchell speaks directly to the preacher who pores over the pages of Scripture each week, looking for inspiration and for an interesting, helpful, fresh idea for a sermon. "Has the Word come alive for me?" is a question that must first be answered in the affirmative. It is through the drama of the preacher's own life that the seeds for sermon ideas begin to take root. On the human level, there is no difference between the one who sits in the pulpit and the one who sits in the pew. Preachers, just like congregants, experience fear, pain, sorrow, and joy. And just as it does for the congregants, the Word meets preachers at the level of their humanness and arrests their attention.

Recently, we observed "Bring a Friend Sunday" at the church where I preach. My text was John 15:12-13, "This is my commandment, that you love one another as I have loved you. Greater love has no one than this, that one lay down one's life for a friend." [2] I believed the text appropriate for the occasion. I was going to talk about Jesus as our friend, loving us with a love so strong that it led him to Calvary. I studied the text. I jotted down notes about Jesus' relationship with all of his disciples, even to the point of highlighting his special friendship with John. But I was still stuck. The sermon was not clicking. My spirit was not grasping the text. I went to bed Saturday night praying God would speak to my spirit before the choir sang the hymn of preparation. Early Sunday morning, my best friend, Joye, called me from New York. We talk to each other daily. Then it hit me like a ton of bricks. I was trying to write a sermon about friendship without talking about my friends.

In my sermon entitled "You Gotta Have Friends: Jesus and Joye," I asked the congregation to "close your eyes and think of one person who you can say without a shadow of a doubt is your best friend. This person may be living or may have already made the eternal transition, but whenever you hear the word 'friend,' their face appears. The person who comes to mind for me is Joye Brown-Toor. We've been friends for twenty-one years. We are very different. She's tall; I'm short. She's slender; I'm . . . short. She's Catholic; I'm Protestant. Joye's idea of fixing her hair is pulling it back with a band; I've sat eight hours to have my hair braided. I wear makeup; she wears lotion. I had to convince her that you do not need anesthesia for a manicure. She had to convince me that it isn't too late to have a happy childhood. We are so different, but we are best friends. One day I found a greater friend than Joye—Jesus."

The next week at least ten members of the church shared how much they were moved by the sermon. One woman said that as she closed her eyes she had envisioned a dear friend who died a few years ago. Tears filled her eyes, but they were tears of joy. In that moment in worship she felt the love of her friend. It was a warm feeling that she carried with her all week long.

Identification Before Entering the Pulpit

Another important tool for preaching to boomers, which is recognized by Henry Mitchell and others, is identification. This concept is exemplified by Ezekiel's experience of being in exile with the children of Israel. In Ezekiel 3:15, the prophet said, "I came to them of the captivity at Telabib, that dwelt by the River of Chebar, and I sat where they sat" (KJV). It is essential that those who preach to the baby boom generation "sit where they sit." Some may think this task difficult or impossible for preachers who are in their twenties or late sixties—not so! Identification makes this possible. Identification is first achieved by listening. Preachers need to become listeners to the stories of the boomers. Listen to their topics of discussion in the barbershop, the beauty shop, the grocery line. What are the subjects designed for them in their magazines (*Time, Newsweek, Essence, Wired,* and *Ebony*)? What are the topics at their conventions, seminars, and retreats? What movies do they attend?

But this is not listening that a preacher does simply to collect bits and pieces for sermon material. Although this may well happen, it is not the goal. The preacher listens to experience what the baby boomers are experiencing; to empathize with their concerns; to allow for their differences; and to improve the intuitive nature of the preacher, relative to this group. Over time, the preacher will gain a window into the souls of those who once seemed a major mystery.

After listening, the preacher must draw a *homiletical road map* from God's story to the stories of the congregants' lives. This road map transports the listeners from the level of their human space to "God's space." God's space is the place where hearers meet a God who (1) cares about them where they are, (2) sits where they sit, and (3) is involved with them on their journey. God's space is a place where the preacher takes the hearers, using images relevant to the hearers' experiences. The preacher can then articulate what God has to say to the hearers about a particular experience or issue.

These relevant images are more than familiar scenery along the journey. They are conduits by which the preacher and the hearer can engage in meaningful exchange. These images make the absent present and decrease the distance between the hearer and the biblical text. Imagination allows the preacher to identify with those in the texts, and then it enables the preacher to introduce the audience to the characters and places he or she has visited. In my tradition the preachers of old used to say, "If I could use my imagination this morning, this is what I would tell you." They were saying to the congregation, "I'm now going to take you on a journey on which you will meet and become familiar with people and places who are centuries removed from you." The result of proper use of imagination in preaching is that the hearers feel they have been there: they experience the text. Imagination places flesh on texts that, without it, are but dry bones in a valley. Abstract theology is not what a person seeking intimacy with God needs to hear on Sunday morning. Mitchell encourages preachers to give so much life to their sermons that the hearers have an "experiential encounter."[3] Another result is that the hearers feel, "You were preaching to *me*." This should be an aim of all preaching.

Practical Preaching and Praxis

Many of today's boomers were reared in the church and left it when it no longer felt relevant to their lives and experiences. Some now have families of their own and have returned to the church seeking spiritual help to deal with the challenges of everyday living. They are looking to the preaching and praxis of the church to guide them through this journey, and also to challenge and give meaning to their lives.

In 2 Timothy 3:16 the apostle Paul tells a young preacher that "all scripture is given by inspiration of God, and is profitable for . . . instruction in righteousness" (KJV). Righteousness is right living. This generation of parents, grandparents, and guardians needs help in guiding the hip-hop generation. Unlike their parents, they need help with children indelibly imprinted by violence, an evaporating American Dream, and an ever-deteriorating ecology. They are demanding a hermeneutic that will take them from the Scripture to their current experiences and moral challenges. They are asking of today's preaching more than their parents asked of the preaching of their generation. We no longer live in a time when the words of the church are accepted as gospel because they were spoken by the preacher.

"Conversion" and "discipleship" are terms that now seem foreign to preachers, who seem content to simply have persons "join the church." Little thought is given, during sermon preparation, to what type of sermon it is that will invite people to accept the suffering servant from Nazareth as their savior and model for life. This is even more obvious when the sermon concludes, and an invitation to join is extended. The preacher may assess numerous things, but often places little emphasis on whether a person is interested in conversion or being a disciple of Christ.

To fail to give attention to a "conversion experience" when preaching to boomers is a critical mistake, especially as it relates to those in the thirty-five to forty-two subgeneration. Although this will be true for persons in both subgenerations, more in the thirty-five to forty-two subgeneration have never held membership in a church and have blurred notions, if any understanding, of concepts such as conversion or discipleship. If we fail in our preaching and pastoral care to help persons rename and embrace these two concepts, of what use is our preaching, teaching, and caring?

Christian bookstores are filled with books and materials designed to reach boomers. These include instructions for creating singles' ministries, couples' ministries, distinctive Bible studies, music ministries, evangelism ministries, and so on. But in these materials, the subjects of conversion and discipleship are noticeably absent, or given sparse attention. Even contemporary homiletic texts tend to focus little on preaching that is concerned with conversion. Others offer esoteric, elitist discussions of discipleship. While a student of Henry H. Mitchell, I was introduced to his concept of preaching for behavioral change.[4] Intellectually the concept made sense. However, it was not until I entered the pastorate that I clearly grasped the critical need to ensure that my sermons were focused to effect behavioral change (conversion, discipleship, forgiveness, honesty, generosity, humility, and so on). After all, it is only by what persons do that the world knows who they are or are not. This is the churchperson's being converted and embarking upon a life of activity that is infused by the Holy Spirit and buttressed by study and participation in the community of faith.

The one who preaches to boomers must not only preach to console and answer questions, she must also preach a prophetic message that persuades hearers to accept the power God gives to implement changes in their lives and the lives of others. This is one of the most important methods through which boomers will gain an understanding of discipleship. It is through living the Word that persons become committed to their faith and gain a better understanding of how it is translated from what they believe in their hearts to what they do with their lives.

N O T E S

1. Henry H. Mitchell, *The Recovery of Preaching* (San Francisco: Harper & Row, 1977), p. 226.
2. *An Inclusive Language Lectionary: Readings for Year B* (Atlanta: John Knox Press; New York: The Pilgrim Press; Philadelphia: Westminster Press; 1984).
3. Henry H. Mitchell, *Celebration and Experience in Preaching* (Nashville: Abingdon Press, 1990), p. 21. See also Mitchell's treatment of experiential encounter discussed in *The Recovery of Preaching* (New York: Harper & Row, 1975), pp. 30-53.
4. Henry H. Mitchell, *Celebration and Experience in Preaching*, pp. 53-60.

CHAPTER THREE

Robert M. Franklin

BEYOND

PREACHING

UNCHURCHED
BLACK MEN

*For African American males in contemporary Amer-*ica, these seem to be the best and the worst of times. Cornel West, Michael Jordan, Colin Powell, and Denzel Washington have attained international stature and admiration. Currently, an African American male, Dr. James Forbes, is pastor of the historic Riverside Church in New York City, where he sets the national standard for excellence in Christian preaching.

At the same time, for too many African American males, life has never been more "nasty, brutish, and short," as the philosopher Thomas Hobbes put it. In recent years, a discouragingly large amount of media attention has fixed upon the melancholic statistics of urban, young African American male existence. Amid trenchant economic uncertainties and a growing sense of personal vulnerability, these reports feed the nation's hunger for culprits and scapegoats.

Perhaps the most ominous of these reports was *Time* magazine's feature story entitled, "Today's Native Sons: Inner-City Black Males are America's Newest Lost Generation."[1] The authors remind us that although African American men comprise about 6 percent of the national population, they constitute half its male prisoners. When the national unemployment rate was 6.9 percent, for African American men it approached 15 percent, and for African American teenagers it was closer to 40 percent. The leading cause of death among African American males between the ages of fifteen and twenty-four is homicide. African American men are increasingly absent from the home, with almost 60 percent of all births to African American women occurring out of wedlock. Finally, the number of African American men enrolled in college is declining rapidly.

Numerous scholars and public leaders have sought to portray the predicament of "today's native sons" as a threat not merely to the future of the African American family and community but to the entire society, thereby making it a cause for concerted public and private action. Speaking to the annual convention of the American Psychological Association, Dr. Joseph N. Gayles Jr., vice president of the Morehouse School of Medicine, said, "It is important for our society to view black male health—both physical and mental—as a major public policy problem and address its solution as a social malignancy affecting . . . the very fabric of American society."[2]

Notwithstanding this catalogue of despair, the public sector has not deemed this state of affairs severe or significant enough to merit intervention. Federal and state government agencies have done little more than expand job opportunities in the military services and construct new prisons to house these problematic citizens.

Regrettably, many religious institutions have exhibited similar ambivalent regard for Black males who fit the underclass profile. In general, churches are more successful in providing ministry to middle-class, educated men. Far from developing innovative and effective outreach ministries to poor men, most African American churches seem to share the wider society's posture of fear, mistrust, impatience, and contempt for them. It would be exceedingly tragic for the African American community and the nation if hundreds of thousands of young African American male lives were to become "wasted treasures" due to the combined effects of structural oppression, personal irresponsibility, and community neglect.

Because religious institutions are the principal zone in which moral values are taught, they have a nonnegotiable obligation to persist in reaching this endangered population who continue to be God's children, no matter how corrupted. Churches, temples, and mosques have done well in the past and must renew their missions with intelligence and urgency. The history of African American home missions work includes stories of breathtaking redemption as manifest in the lives of persons such as Malcolm X, as well as the common story of millions of unnamed men who were empowered to resist and overcome the traumas of oppression.

In my judgment, the crisis of the African American male in America is fundamentally, although not exclusively, a spiritual one. I am using the term *spiritual* to refer to an ensemble of features including a human being's basic sense of personhood in relation to an ultimate concern, commonly named God. The spiritual dimension is the locus of a person's most fundamental values and commitments, that internal center that is the source of love and the hopeful affirmation of life and the future. From this realm springs forth the human longing for truth, goodness, and beauty in the world. In the African American community, spirituality has been understood to be a holistic style of living, which is attentive to both the personal and the social dimensions and qualities of wholeness and justice.

To be sure, the spiritual crisis of African American men has other significant dimensions—political, economic, cultural. But throughout history African American men have suffered the indignity of deprivation in each of these zones without losing hope, defiance, spirit, collective purpose, and confidence in God. Following the analysis of sociologist William Julius Wilson, I am suggesting that something new has occurred in the modern, post–Civil Rights movement era. In the opening passage of his book *The Truly Disadvantaged: The Inner City, the Underclass, and Public Policy,* Wilson characterizes the contrast between the past and present:

> In the mid-1960s, urban analysts began to speak of a *new dimension to the urban crisis* in the form of a large subpopulation of low-income families and individuals whose behavior contrasted sharply with the behavior of the general population. Despite a high rate of poverty in ghetto neighborhoods throughout the first half of

the twentieth century, rates of inner-city joblessness, teenage pregnancies, out-of-wedlock births, female-headed families, welfare dependency, and serious crime were significantly lower than in later years and did not reach *catastrophic proportions until the mid-1970s.*[3] (Italics mine)

It is important to remember that the current internal, spiritual crisis of which I speak is linked inextricably to broader national and global trends, such as this nation's economic slip into postindustrial decline; the retreat of the federal government from funding and properly monitoring social welfare programs; a growing malaise, initiated by the Watergate revelations, concerning public morality; the infusion of narcotics into urban centers, matched with the gradual tolerance of drug use and drug marketing in many communities; and the devastating effects of the Vietnam War upon the collective American consciousness. Together, this ensemble of social ills conspired to "reexpose the spiritual, economic and political chaos existent in the African American community," and highlighted the inability or "failure of the church in recent history to respond significantly to those conditions."[4]

Crisis means decision. At stake here are nothing less than the souls of African American menfolk. Will they reclaim the inner resources necessary to resist the onslaughts of injustice, domination, depression, and weariness? Or will they succumb to the nearly overwhelming forces of destruction?

As we approach a new century, this spiritual challenge will be so monumental that those who survive will require a dynamic amalgam of spiritual, moral, cognitive, and behavioral resources that can be found most readily in the great faith traditions, especially Christianity and traditional African religions.

In *Black Men*, the late Dr. James S. Tinney presents a brief but insightful synopsis of "The Religious Experience of Black Men" (though he does not address the experience of non-Christian men). He argues that the African American church is a male institution, because some men (particularly clergy) have benefited positively from it, especially in terms of leadership development, psychological liberation, intellectual growth, financial reward, and encouragement of male authority in the home. But for most laymen, the story is very different. Indeed, he noted that "many black males seem uninterested in, or hostile to, the African American church."[5] A slight overstatement would be that the church is female space owned and operated by men.

While preparing a master's thesis at Harvard, I tried to account for the paradox cited by Tinney. Through a series of group interviews, I recorded African American males' explanations for their exodus from the church. The explanations included the following institutional factors: (1) the social teachings of Christianity encouraged passivity and meekness—traits that are dysfunctional in street culture; (2) the image of the moral person embraced in the churches is comprised of a disproportionate number of so-called feminine character traits, such as quiescence, humility, nonassertiveness, and self-sacrifice, that repel men in pursuit of machismo; (3) since the Civil Rights movement, most churches have withdrawn from vigorous social activism and have turned attention to institutional expansion and physical improvement; (4) even when involved in politics, churches are insufficiently radical and prophetic in their political orientations, choosing to support rather than fight the powers that be; (5) worship in the churches tends to be excessively long and often thematically unintelligible; (6) the dominant religious symbols of the church are problematic either in expressing devotion to Eurocentric aesthetic values (the Nordic Christ) or in failing to adequately portray African American life in racist America; (7) churches are preoccupied with fund-raising and tend to be insensitive to poor people; (8) churches seem to tolerate obvious hypocrisy among valued members while inducing excessive guilt among ordinary folk, especially in relation to sexuality and recreational drug or alcohol use.

Although a growing number of progressive clergy and congregations are working to correct many of these items, in general, the churches have not changed significantly. These "exodus explanations" are still valid for many men, albeit less prominent than during the 1960s and mid-1970s. By the end of the 1970s and the beginning of the 1980s, significant developments occurring generally within society and specifically within the African American community resulted in increased religious participation among males. Together, these related social forces created a *push/pull* dynamic from which churches and other religious institutions benefited.

First, the repressive economic and racial climate (and policies fostered by the administrations of Presidents Reagan and Bush) *pushed* many African American men back into religious institutions, searching for community support and answers to tough life questions. A similar phenomenon may occur as the Republican-headed Congress scales down support for poor people. Second, reforms within the African American church initiated by a new generation of sophisticated Black clergy who were products of the Black liberation theology movement *pulled* many disaffected African American men into the churches. We should not equate mere church attendance with the inner transformation that must occur for personal wholeness. But reaffiliation with a community of faith is an important first step in claiming one's identity as a member of a community of hope, struggle, and accountability. If this phenomenon continues, it could offer some hope for the religious regeneration of African American men and the heightened vigor of African American church ministries to them.

Since preaching was and is central to ministries provided by these products of the Black liberation theology movement, it is important to examine the nature of this preaching. What has made it palatable? Why does it have the power to draw those who had exited or who had never darkened the church doors? This type of preaching has at least three central features: theological content, socioeconomic analysis, and moral challenge.

Theological Content: A God Who Is Not Color-Blind

Among the exodus explanations I cited earlier, two are particularly important at this juncture. First, the dominant religious symbols of the church are problematic in either expressing devotion to Eurocentric aesthetic values (the Nordic Christ) or in failing adequately portray African American life in racist America. Second, worship in the churches tends to be excessively long and often thematically unintelligible.

The preacher who is reaching men who were once a part of the exodus movement preaches about a God who is not color-blind. This God celebrates the identity of Black men and affirms their Blackness. This God is not a God who is indifferent to race and ethnicity. This is important for men whose daily experience is marked by either the negation of or stigmatization based on race. These are men who have often asked themselves, Of those with the power to alter the status quo, who cares? Most of America does not seem to care. Neither the government, the school system, corporate America, nor the media seem to care. Many middle-class African Americans seem indifferent. Who cares? So to hear that the One who has "all power" embraces them and affirms who they are is, on an ontological level, profoundly healing and uplifting.

This new generation of preachers is unapologetically Afrocentric. They realize that sound preaching is more than exegeting a text; the preacher must also be able to exegete the congregation. Their themes are intelligible. They strike a chord with these brothers. They evoke sounds from the amen corner because the preaching is relevant to the experiences of the listeners. For years these exodus men have heard sermons that speak of a God who rules a pluralistic society where all major differences are insignificant. They have been told that since God is no respecter of persons, this is the order of the day. But as they daily live out an existence in which their skin color is most often a factor that mitigates against them, they long for a God who knows. Surely God must know that they do not live in a pluralistic society. Surely God must care about this dilemma. Surely God must have a Word that speaks to this reality. And how will they hear it without a preacher?

Preaching and the Socioeconomic Analysis

The second central feature of this preaching is its ability to articulate the depth of rage that Black men feel. Psychoanalysts remind us of the ego defense mechanism wherein anger masks pain. For most men I know, anger is easier (in other words, more socially acceptable) to express than pain. But even here, there is a racial double standard. Whereas racism permits White men to be angry with impunity, it ensures that African American male rage is carefully monitored, suppressed, and punished. Because anger must be properly channeled to be of benefit, this along with the racism of America provides a great challenge for preaching.

Three other exodus explanations are relevant here. First, the social teachings of Christ, as presented in years past, encouraged passivity and meekness, which are dysfunctional in street culture. Second, since the Civil Rights movement, most churches have withdrawn from vigorous social activism and have turned their attention to institutional expansion and physical improvement. Third, even when involved in politics, churches are insufficiently radical and prophetic in their political orientation, choosing to support rather than fight the powers that be. In light of these explanations, the preacher who can articulate the depth of the rage of Black men will be heard.

The social justice movement, for which we once lauded the Black church, has long since died or at best hibernated. Articulating the depth of the rage of Black folk is an expansion of the social justice agenda of the Black church. This new preaching is explicit about society's responsibility for the plight of Black men. It says that the police transgress, not only against Black men who commit crimes, but also against those who do not. It points out the transgressions of the government concerning jobs and education. Once the demon is named, then and only then is there a sense that one can challenge the demon. Then and only then can the demon be cast out. Those who have suffered at the hands of the demon have known with certainty that they were sane—that social evil was not a figment of their imagination. This capricious cruelty was real, but the church was not saying, "Amen, brothers: You're right."

This is the type of preaching that came forth from Malcolm X, who understood and diagnosed African American self-hatred, hurt, and rage with brilliant clarity and force. This is the type of preaching that launched Jesse Jackson to national prominence in the 1970s. It is the type of preaching at which Louis Farrakhan currently is more adept. Thus in spite of the flaws in aspects of Farrakhan's message, a million Black people went when he called. They went because they know the parts of his message that are true, deeply true. They went because, among other reasons, they wanted to hear a preacher say that America is scarred by the sin of racism but it can be healed—that the Supreme Court and the lower courts do not believe in equal rights, and that social justice is something few Black men can expect to receive. This new preaching emphasizes that it is the role of the preacher to help keep warriors fit for duty so that they can oppose the enemy who is real.

Those who truly articulate the depth of the rage of Black men are honest about the social and economic landscape of America. They preach that the glass ceiling is real. "Yes," they say, "we can overcome." But first they say, "Brothers, it will be difficult, and I'm honestly going to tell you why." They preach that Malcolm X is still right. In America, large segments of White society still refer to a Black man with a Ph.D. as a nigger if he attempts to live out all his unalienable rights. His own status is jeopardized if he tries to bring others along as he climbs. They preach that most often, despite his skill, a Black man will earn less than his White counterpart. If he makes progress in leveling the playing field, though the progress is slight, he may be sued for reverse discrimination or silenced through other means. The preacher to the exodus men is honest enough to say that seven generations after slavery, the options for the average African American man in America are the same as those of their foreparents.

Moral Challenge Presented by These Preachers

The third feature that characterizes this preaching is the empowering invitation to action. It brings together the theological and the social and extends an opportunity to act. This occurs because the preaching shows a new empathy for the frustration and the potential of these men whom society has discarded. The preachers show this through preaching that is sometimes autobiographical. In their vulnerability they reveal themselves to be preachers who also have faults. They too have been prodigal sons and daughters; they too have scars from being in the wrong place, from doing the wrong thing, and from being in a place doing nothing at all. They are not perfect men and women who preach to point fingers at others. They possess the type of empathy that elicits trust.

Although these preachers have shown vulnerability before in the pulpit, many from the exodus group have written it off as hypocritical. This seems to have been due, in large part, to another explanation: that churches seem to tolerate obvious hypocrisy among valued members while inducing excessive guilt among ordinary folk, especially in relation to sexuality and recreational drug or alcohol use.

But this show of vulnerability by the new era preachers is tempered by the requirement that they also be people who are respectable or on the road toward respectability. They are preachers whom others can believe because their lives show that they understand that moral betterment is essential for our collective good. Henry Mitchell, through his actions, has taught me that orthodoxy must be reinforced by orthopraxis.

Once the community affirms these men as valuable members, they can actualize their potential as parents, contributors, and leaders. Men who are loved, who properly love themselves, will not dehumanize women or show indifference toward children. As men are reintegrated into the religious community and develop new self-respect, self-esteem, and responsibility, they can do much to overcome and reconcile strained social and family relationships.

As we stand on the brink of decision we are witnessing a new era of Black urban preaching that has the capacity to effect redemption and reconciliation within and among African American men and their loved ones. This is a time for celebration and renewed dedication to speak and do the truth while time permits. We cannot fail our brother, for if we do, we fail ourselves.

N O T E S

1. Jacob V. Lamar Jr. et al., "Today's Native Sons," *Time*, 1 December 1986, pp. 26-29.
2. Dr. Joseph N. Gayles Jr., quoted in Ann Hardie, "Problems Facing Black Men Threaten U.S. Society, Psychologists Say," *Atlanta Constitution*, Monday, 15 August 1988, sec. D.
3. William Julius Wilson, *The Truly Disadvantaged: The Inner City, the Underclass, and Public Policy* (Chicago: University of Chicago Press, 1987), p. 3.
4. This statement was made in 1993 by Dean Clarence Newsome of the Howard University School of Divinity. He was the responder for my lecture on explanations for exodus of African American males from the church.
5. James S. Tinney, "The Religious Experience of Black Men," in *Black Men*, ed. Lawrence E. Gary (Beverly Hills: Sage, 1981), pp. 269-76.
6. See Henry H. Mitchell and Emil M. Thomas, *Preaching for Black Self Esteem* (Nashville: Abingdon Press, 1994); Henry H. Mitchell, *Black Preaching* (Philadelphia and New York: J. B. Lippincott, 1970); and Henry H. Mitchell and Nicholas Cooper-Lewter, *Soul Theology* (San Francisco: Harper & Row, 1986; reprint, Nashville: Abingdon Press, 1991). These writings speak volumes to what preachers can preach and do to help African American males.

PART TWO

WHAT IS
BEING
HEARD?

CHAPTER FOUR

Eugene L. Lowry

PREACHING
THE GREAT
THEMES

*W*hen one remembers Henry Mitchell's insistence on behavioral objectives, preaching as folk culture, and "gut level" communication, "Preaching the Great Themes" at first seems an unlikely topic with which to further a discussion about the substance of the preached Word. Although Mitchell once noted that "great celebration is only generated by the treatment of great themes,"[1] nonetheless, the term "great themes" relative to preaching may easily evoke the sensibility of a different era, a different style, and certainly a different cultural and economic base than that from which Mitchell preached.

I remember the "great theme preaching" that I heard in my early adulthood. The time was post–World War II and before the Korean conflict. Times were good for many of us: the economy was rolling onward and upward, White male graduates expected and generally found jobs that fit their training; White women found the work for which they had been socialized; positive expectations and confident affirmations were the daily messages of politicians; and churches were full of renewed enthusiasm for what I later learned to call "civil religion." The pulpit was topical, privatistic, and optimistic—full of Enlightenment-style hopefulness regarding knowledge and will. Generally there would be a biblical text to buttress the good advice. Jesus was portrayed as a wonderful model for "high road" living.

To be sure, had I been fortunate enough to have listened in on the National Radio Pulpit or the Lutheran Hour, I would have been offered a far more expansive theological menu. Clearly, a Ralph Sockman, a David H. C. Read, a Robert J. McCracken, or an Edwin T. Dahlberg would have had quite different understandings of what constitutes "great themes." Even so, the emerging commonalities of sermon structure, biblical hermeneutic, and social science affinity during this period are striking.

The North American pulpit was shifting from expository to topical preaching. Harry Emerson Fosdick, himself accused (falsely, I think) of being a psychologizing topical preacher,[2] warned that often those who rebelled against expository preaching "searched contemporary life in general and the newspapers in particular for subjects." Instead of concentrating on textual analysis, they dealt with present-day themes about which everyone was thinking. Instead of launching out from a great text they started with their own opinions on some matter of current interest, often much farther away than a good biblical text would be from the congregation's vital concerns and needs.[3] They seemed not to hear any echo of a Barth suggesting that when and if you get to the Bible with your deepest longings, the first biblical response likely will be: "*Nein*, wrong question."[4]

Perhaps most striking of the times was the cerebral—that is, left-brain cerebral—modality of White male preaching that "would seem to imply a primarily intellectual target," says Mitchell, "with the homiletic skills sought and taught focusing on the production of a stimulating idea."[5] In an early writing, Mitchell quotes Alan Geyer of the *Christian Century* to explain that (in 1969) "Systematic theology, by and large, remains in a state of Teutonic captivity."[6]

The homiletical consequence in the White congregation, Mitchell explains, is a rather limited (sometimes even emotionless) appeal directed to a very thin band of rationality. In great contrast to this is the sermon preached within the Black culture, which, he says, "has not progressed to the level of this lofty and ancient mistake."[7]

All of which is to say that when confronted by the phrase "preaching the great themes," many of us are not likely to think of Henry Mitchell as an eager proponent. Yet, such a case can be made—*if* one utilizes several crucial determining variables.

Word/World Juxtaposition

The first variable has to do with different kinds of answers to the question of the relation of gospel to human existence. Comparing Fosdick to Barth, for example, will help identify the issue. Fosdick worked on the assumption of continuity of Word to world. His homiletical method was based on the premise that the preacher takes a situation, whether personal or corporate, local or international, and presses it by illustration and argument until it is ripe for intersection with the gospel—"the garnered wisdom of all ages"[8]—by which he means the Word drawn from the canon. Note the fit of issue and answer, operating by a transforming continuity.

Barth, on the other hand, wanted no part of a religion that "answers" our needs. An utter transformation of the question by negation is the only means of positioning by which God might address us with the Word. Says Barth, "If the congregation brings to church the great question of human life and seeks an answer for it, the Bible contrariwise brings an answer, and seeks the question corresponding to this answer."[9] Such utter discontinuity! As Paul Scherer would put it, the preacher should not seek to meet the listener where the listener is because "too often he is in the wrong place."[10]

The consideration of "great themes" has to be remarkably different in these two traditions—one affirming yet transforming, and the other negating and subsequently radically reformulating. Moreover, when the issue of Word/world juxtaposition is addressed in the context of African American culture, it becomes complicated by two factors. On the one hand, Henry Mitchell notes the similarities of the West African religious tradition and the tradition of the Hebrew Scriptures, specifically including "a High God who was omnipotent, omniscient, and just," and, hence, a tradition that strongly affirmed the "goodness of life." On the other hand, "Blacks here in America soon found a level of evil they never dreamed of."[11]

Mitchell's understanding of both the goodness of life and also the unbelievable evil in living finds compatible connections with the views of both Fosdick and Barth. Mitchell surely shares Fosdick's confidence in the power of great biblical themes to connect with the people. "Preaching must speak to the human condition," beginning by focusing "on a sensitive living issue."[12] Yet at the same time he must share something of that sense of the radicality of evil that Barth called "a worse abyss"[13] than we could dream.

Given these factors, Mitchell's position is that the sermon must provide "the establishment of a celebrative island of consciousness in an ocean of oppression and deprivation."[14] As Mitchell explains: "Black Americans have come through trials and tribulations of suicidal proportions, and they have kept on living when others would have given up long since, simply because they have been fed on [such great themes as] the justice, mercy, goodness and providence of the Creator." In short, "Great celebration is only generated by the treatment of great themes."[15]

The potential power of preaching and celebrating the great themes is maximized, then, by the longing context of the "as if," the "not yet," the "in spite of" reality of a presently unrealized eschatology.

Juxtaposition becomes the critical key here. For example, the juxtaposition of the biblical theme of the goodness of creation with the current mean state of affairs in the United States provides a collision that offers the great potential for powerful preaching.

Walter Brueggemann expresses this point magnificently in *The Prophetic Imagination*. The torque of juxtaposition between the royal consciousness and the alternative consciousness can be evoked by means of preaching the great themes of alternative consciousness that are otherwise silenced by a cover-up. So, Brueggemann makes it clear, "The royal consciousness leads people to numbness, especially to numbness about death. It is the task of prophetic ministry and imagination to bring people to engage their experiences of suffering to death."[16]

Transconscious Connection

The second variable with which Mitchell and great theme preaching connect is his understanding of transconsciousness. A term drawn from Mircea Eliade, with some connections to the work of Jung and

James, the term "transconsciousness" refers to "vast collections of responses and values in the less-charted sectors of consciousness, invisibly and largely inaccessibly stored."[17] Apparently, his attention was drawn to this idea by his study of the various levels and stages of relationship between African American espousal of Christianity and the religious traditions of Africa.

Mitchell explains that "the earlier Greek dichotomy of flesh and spirit was perhaps only made worse by the Enlightenment, which added reason-vs.-feeling to the division of the human psyche."[18] The net result, according to Mitchell, is a failure of the typical White sermon to reach the whole person.

Because African Americans missed the Western dualism, Black preaching is able to engage the whole person.[19] In particular, the use of metaphor and image can tap the reservoir of the transconscious levels of knowing, and hence access the deep places of knowing where "reorganization of the image,"[20] as Kenneth Boulding once put it, or the "shock of recognition,"[21] as Fred Craddock described it, might occur with transforming power.

Says Mitchell, "The goal of Black preaching is to recreate a meaningful experience which communicates transconsciously, nourishing the whole human being. This is indeed high art."[22] Surely this is the goal of all preaching.

Biblical Narration

The third factor crucial to great theme preaching is narrative form and content. The "great theme" preaching I heard growing up tended to be topical universals defined, rather than storied events described. Universals tend toward bland ideation; events carry enfleshed particularity. For example, "Forgiveness" must have been considered a great theme, since we heard about it so frequently. "Discipleship" was big during my college days. (Of the "great theme" preaching I can recall from my youth, the only sermons that seemed to be enfleshed came from a preacher we had during my early school days. He was big on "Temptation," and it was always enfleshed.) "Growth in Grace" is certainly a theme ever looming large in tradition—with matters often explained theologically, yet seldom enfleshed in storied fashion.

Perhaps these preachers had not read H. Richard Niebuhr's *The Meaning of Revelation*, in which he notes that the preaching of the early church did not focus on metaphysical generalities, but rather was "primarily a simple recital of the great events [that] happened to the community of disciples."[23] Likewise, Mitchell is not interested in Enlightenment-style universal truths. He is interested in "eye witness" accounts. "If you have an idea that can't be translated into a story or picture," says Mitchell, "don't use it."[24] Moreover, "One cannot generate a rerun of an experience one has never had personally nor appropriated."[25]

When Mitchell speaks of preaching great themes, he means great *biblical* themes—that are peopled with biblical characters who in fact have contemporary counterparts. "The story must be internalized in the preacher, peopled by characters . . . known for years and for whom [there are] such deep feelings that [the preacher] can authentically recreate the action and communicate the experience."[26]

He claims that "in every Black Bible story, there must be a plot, with characters and conflict." Likewise, he notes that "there must be suspense—curiosity as to the outcome of the conflict right up to the end."[27] Sometimes the sermon builds like a symphonic orchestration, notes Melva Wilson Costen. "One can wait in anticipation of an adagio movement, which could gradually build up to a scherzo celebration, or a sonata allegro form with numerous recapitulations and a lengthy coda."[28]

But sometimes the biblical passage does not have a story line. It may be a grocery list of Christian qualities. Even here, advises Mitchell, it must be plotted. "It may be a wholly imaginary conflict, with Grace or Mercy as the protagonist and the law as the opponent, for example." In whatever type of situation, the "imagination is called upon . . . to establish a plot and a convincing eyewitness account."[29]

These three variables—Word/world juxtaposition, transconscious connection, and biblical narration—serve to energize, even revolutionize great theme preaching.

In their book *Soul Theology*, Henry H. Mitchell and Nicholas Cooper-Lewter discuss great themes drawn from "the heart of American Black culture." They are the following: "the providence of God"; "the justice of God"; "the majesty and omnipotence of God"; "the omniscience of God"; "the goodness of God and creation"; "the grace of God"; "the equality of persons"; "the uniqueness of persons: identity"; "the family of God and humanity"; and "the perseverance of persons."

No one should be surprised that the discussion of each of these themes commences with a biblical text. Nor should we fail to note that these great themes are set in the context of ambiguity, tension, or torque born of Word/world juxtaposition, transconscious connection, and biblical narration. The chapter titled "The Providence of God," for example, establishes the juxtaposition of Romans 8:28—"And we know that God works in everything for good"—with the spiritual "Nobody Knows the Trouble I See." In discussing "the goodness of God and creation," Mitchell and Cooper-Lewter observe that "Blacks have praised God for centuries, throughout the darkest moments of slavery, by celebrating the smallest blessings from God." The transconscious connection of the "Gospel Train" spiritual ("the fare is cheap, and all can ride") undergirds the discussion of "the equality of persons."[30]

As I imagine the next century—considering its potential for good and ill—three great themes emerge in my mind repeatedly. Put negatively, the interrelated issues are violence, instrumentalism, and the "law of the jungle." Positively stated, the biblically based great themes must include the vision of *shalom*, the intrinsic dignity of persons, and the gift and claim of community. The variables of Word/world juxtaposition, transconscious connection, and biblical narration become enfleshed in the particulars of these themes, and hence serve here to illustrate their energizing power.

Presently, for example, we are moving ever more clearly into a chronic cultural mood of violence—primarily located not with the overt act but with the underlying spirit of contempt for anyone or anything standing in one's own way. Only a vision of *shalom* can bring relief, transforming, as it does, the way the world deals with difference.

Likewise, a broad and base utilitarianism pervades our world; we seem not to understand any sacred center, but rather surf for pragmatic possibilities. Dignity born of intrinsic values and growing out of the biblical revelation becomes an incredibly crucial theme. In both Hebraic and African cultures, the nondualistic, transconscious connections of existence can be sensed at a deeper than conscious level of awareness.

In a society where the rich are getting not only richer, but also meaner and more myopic, while the poor are getting poorer, we need to name the gospel's claim of community neither earned nor planned but created by divine gift. The story of that divine gift is at the heart of biblical narration.

The principle in the handling of all these themes (or any other for that matter) is captured nicely by this volume's title: *Preaching on the Brink*. Not only is it true that we are at the brink of a new century; it is also true that preaching great themes always means preaching on the brink.

Powerful preaching never consists simply of announcing some obvious conclusion, or naming some clear virtues, or capturing some divine certainty. The powerful sermon happens on the brink, the edge, the almost, the verge, the border. The torque of Word/world juxtaposition, the border of transconscious connection, and the parabolic verge of biblical narration are all principal participants in the dynamics of preaching on the brink.

We preach the great themes expectantly, preaching at the boundary called Promise and leaning on the edge called Hope.

N O T E S

1. Henry H. Mitchell, *The Recovery of Preaching* (San Francisco: Harper & Row, 1977), p. 59.
2. See Harry Emerson Fosdick, *A Great Time to Be Alive* (New York: Pocket Books, 1954), pp. 139-46.
3. Harry Emerson Fosdick, *The Living of These Days* (New York: Harper & Bros., 1956), pp. 92-93.
4. See Karl Barth, *The Word of God and the Word of Man* (New York: Harper & Bros., 1956), pp. 28-50. "The Strange New World Within the Bible"
5. Mitchell, *The Recovery of Preaching*, p. 12.
6. Henry H. Mitchell, *Black Preaching* (Philadelphia and New York: J. B. Lippincott, 1970), p. 23, quoting Alan Geyer, "Toward a Convivial Theology," *The Christian Century* 86, no. 17 (23 April 1969), p. 542.
7. Mitchell, *The Recovery of Preaching*, p. 13.
8. Fosdick, *The Living of These Days*, p. 5.
9. Barth, *The Word of God and the Word of Man*, p. 116
10. Paul Scherer, *The Word God Sent* (New York: Harper & Row, 1965), p. 7.
11. Mitchell, *The Recovery of Preaching*, pp. 18-19.
12. Ibid., p. 142.
13. Barth, *The Word of God and the Word of Man*, p. 117.
14. Mitchell, *The Recovery of Preaching*, p. 57.
15. Ibid., p. 59.
16. Walter Brueggemann, *The Prophetic Imagination* (Philadelphia: Fortress Press, 1978), p. 46.
17. Mitchell, *The Recovery of Preaching*, p. 14.
18. Ibid., p. 13.

19. Ibid., see p. 12.
20. Kenneth E. Boulding, *The Image* (Ann Arbor: The University of Michigan, 1956), p. 8.
21. Fred B. Craddock, *Preaching* (Nashville: Abingdon Press, 1985), p. 160.
22. Mitchell, *The Recovery of Preaching*, p. 33.
23. H. Richard Niebuhr, *The Meaning of Revelation* (New York: Macmillan, 1941), p. 32.
24. Mitchell, *The Recovery of Preaching*, p. 45.
25. Ibid., p. 34.
26. Ibid., p. 37.
27. Mitchell, *Black Preaching*, p. 136.
28. Melva Wilson Costen, *African American Christian Worship* (Nashville: Abingdon Press, 1993), p. 105.
29. Mitchell, *Black Preaching*, p. 136.
30. Nicholas Cooper-Lewter and Henry H. Mitchell, *Soul Theology* (San Francisco: Harper & Row, 1986; reprint, Nashville: Abingdon Press, 1991), pp. 14-15, 67-68, 96-99.

CHAPTER FIVE

Fred B. Craddock

I S T H E R E

S T I L L R O O M

F O R R H E T O R I C ?

*T*his question is for preaching a very serious one. It asks whether or not the marriage between homiletics and rhetoric should be terminated. Because the marriage has been such a long one, respect for history demands there be no divorce without careful reflection. Formally speaking, it was Augustine who officiated at the wedding joining the rhetorical principles of Cicero to the growing and changing ministry of preaching. The informal homilies of house churches[1] had given way to lofty pulpits before large audiences. The government had given the Christians a public voice. Augustine taught the church how to preach so as to be persuasive: appeal to the mind (What is the message?), the heart (How does it affect my life?), and the will (What am I to do?).

Even though Augustine is properly credited with providing the first "textbook" in homiletics, it should be pointed out that the use of rhetoric in communicating the gospel is a practice at least as old as the New Testament itself. Rhetorical critical approaches to the biblical texts have been fruitful in yielding fresh understandings of writers, readers, cultural contexts, and social locations. For example, the Letter to the Hebrews, which is by its own designation a sermon ("word of exhortation," 13:22 NRSV), employs many rhetorical strategies: alliteration, repetition, inclusion, refrain, contrast, double negative, multiple nouns without conjunctions, use of nouns as adjectives, and others. In fact, rhetoric so dominated the curricula of academics in the ancient Mediterranean world that it was almost impossible for public communication, oral and written, to be free of it. Recent rhetorical approaches to biblical texts have made us aware of how widely these skills were used, and in the process have opened up new understandings of the writers, their readers, and their social locations.

Augustine's adaptation of rhetoric for preaching came to America and dominated the study and practice of homiletics well into the twentieth century. The most popular textbook in preaching from the late nineteenth until the middle of this century was John Broadus's *On the Preparation and Delivery of Sermons.* Broadus laid out the ancient pattern of persuasion: What is it? What is its worth? How do I get it? However, by the 1960s this rhetorical structure for sermons noticeably declined in influence. There were two primary reasons for this. First, the method collapsed under the weight of its own popularity. Congregations were being served sermons in three parts every Sunday (even though often the intent was not to persuade and the three parts were not appeals to mind, heart, and will). Whatever the text, whatever the subject, sermons had three points. Sadly, as is often the case with practices born of worthy purpose and rich with history, Cicero's contribution to homiletics fell subject to jokes about "three points and a poem." Second, the pulpit of the 1960s and beyond faced a barrage of questions that, in the attempts to answer by both church and academy, brought about major changes in the study and practice of preaching. There were questions about the preacher, questions concerning authority and the right to persuade others to his or her position rather than facilitating a conversation between the community and its Scriptures. There were questions about the use of text: Should not the forms of texts be honored in the sermon rather than forcing all texts to fit a three-point grid? And perhaps most important, questions about the listeners: Do they not deserve the right to be more active participants in the sermon, completing thoughts, taking alternate positions, drawing their own conclusions? Does the priesthood of believers not apply to preaching? After all, the message belongs as much to them as to the preacher.

The old consensus about sermons has been broken. Homileticians no longer agree that the sole purpose of the sermon is to persuade and to do so by a single form of reasoning. But one does not close the door on so major a contributor to preaching without asking, Is there still room for rhetoric? Several responses are appropriate. First, *decisions about the continued role of rhetoric in preaching should not be unduly influenced by the current cynicism about all uses of language.* It is no coincidence that claims about the emptiness and impotence of language come at a time when values are abandoned and morals are eroded.[2] Words and values are inseparably related, and for the pulpit to acquiesce in one is to acquiesce in the other. The preacher, more than any other person in our society, struggles against the degeneration of speech into irresponsible and confusing sounds. The preacher is a keeper of the church's vocabulary, vigilant in maintaining the integrity of words and the Word. Pulpits caught up in postmodern doubts about language will fall silent.

Second, *preaching cannot permit itself to be intimidated by the popular use of the word* rhetoric *in a pejorative sense.* Often one hears the expression "empty rhetoric": that is, words without substance, speech designed to give the impression of sincerity and truth but which, in fact, lacks both. John Milton, in *Paradise Lost,* described the cunning Belial as the master rhetorician: his tongue dropped manna, he pleased the ear, he spoke with persuasive accents. Such depreciation of rhetoric is as old as Plato, who regarded it as verbal artifice designed to manipulate the masses, dazzle the ignorant, and give the appearance of reason when there was none. So pervasive are such suspicions about rhetoric that a broad segment of our society regards an articulate person as less honest than the person with awkward speech. This accounts for the politicians skilled at appearing unskilled in their pursuit of voters. The outrages committed by articulate speakers against unsuspecting audiences, often with tragic consequences, have been so well-chronicled that the preacher does well not only to be self-critical but also to be continually engaged with colleagues in discussing the ethics of public speaking.

But again, violations of one's art should not intimidate one into silence. Rhetoric is not by its nature off-limits for the sincere and caring preacher. According to Aristotle, "Rhetoric may be defined as the faculty of observing in any given case the available means of persuasion."[3]

Aristotle's definition involves two movements: the investigation into the heart of a matter and the arrangement of the materials related to that matter so as to move an audience to judge, to decide, to approve, or to disapprove. Three factors enter into the rhetorical occasion: the character of the speaker, the subject matter, and the disposition of the hearers. Nothing here subverts the high seriousness of preaching. All this is to say that an answer to the question, "Is there still room for rhetoric?" should draw upon the best teachers and practitioners of homiletics and not upon clever abusers of the art.

This second response to our title question brings us naturally to a third: *Any consideration of the use of rhetoric must first deal with the prior question of persuasion.* This is to say, Is it the business of preaching to persuade others? After all, rhetoric is about persuasion. Both "Of course" and "Of course not" are poor answers if given too soon. Anyone entering the preaching ministry needs to ponder the fundamental question of what one wants to happen during and after a sermon.[4] Some have a strong hesitation about being instrumental in changing the lives of others. Therefore, sermons are prepared and delivered with no expectation of anything happening or with perhaps even a fear that somebody may be changed. Such sermons may be given in the belief that "Truth is its own evangelist" and all the preachers have to do is transmit the information. If, however, as a result of such preaching someone alters relationships, or ways of getting and spending money, or vocation, or view of the world, then the preacher may claim the truth is solely responsible and the messenger is not an accessory in the disruption of anyone's lifestyle. Or sermons may be designed to say absolutely nothing that might make a difference, or to be so boring that apathy is virtually guaranteed. Some preachers may not be conscious of such pulpit behavior, but it is not uncommon, given the rhetorical timidity of those who question their right to persuade. And understandably, there is for many the very real fear of taking unfair advantage of the listeners. Some are very sensitive about participating in what they regard as a conspiracy: sacred Scripture, sacred desk, and sacred service "gang up" on the hearers. Is there available to the audience a reasonable and respectable alternative to a silent acquiescence to the message? Is saying no to a sermon saying no to God? Can a yes be a valid response if the possibility of a no is denied?

Let the preacher return again and again to these questions. Of course we all seek to persuade others, in our families, at work, in politics, in the church, but we do not attempt to do so from a "bully pulpit." Of course we employ rhetorical strategies appropriate to both subject matter and occasion, but we do not do so in order to silence other voices, other views. We seek to persuade, yes, but to persuade the silent to claim their voices, the powerless to stand and be counted, the dependent to take responsibility for their own faith, the fearful to risk and to trust. And especially do we employ all the rhetoric available to persuade the church to engage the Scriptures for itself rather than accepting weekly reports on what the preacher discovered there. When that healthy condition prevails, the persuaders will sometimes find themselves being persuaded.

One final word about persuasion: let us not assume that, because most preaching is to the church, persuasion is inappropriate. Presence in a sanctuary does not mean that a person is a believer informed in the faith and a firm disciple of Jesus. There are many reasons for showing up on Sunday, and one of them is to inquire. With Christendom long dead and pluralism very much alive, this is hardly the time for a rhetorical retreat, offering value-free discourses, void of any hint of advocacy. Christian faith listens with a willingness to be changed by what is heard, but Christian faith also takes its turn at the podium.

A fourth and final response to the question, Is there still room for rhetoric? is offered as a suggestion. *Rather than debating the merits of rhetorical preaching as fashioned by Cicero, adapted by Augustine, and mediated through John Broadus, let us broaden our understanding of rhetoric.* Biblical scholars are reading the handbooks of ancient Greek and Latin rhetoricians, making discoveries that shed light on the achievement of the writers of Scripture. Let us do the same, being instructed in our task by these masters of communication: Aristotle, Cicero, Quintilian, and Isocrates.

A few examples may serve to support this suggestion. The prevailing pattern of traditional preaching in America has been deductive. This is to say, a theme or proposition was stated and from that general truth the sermon drew particular implications and applications. For audiences who accepted the preacher's major premise, the opening proposition, such preaching moved smoothly and persuasively. In support of this deductive reasoning, the name of Aristotle was invoked, and properly so. In his *Rhetoric* Aristotle developed in detail the manner and merits of this form of argumentation. It was natural, therefore, for those preachers and homileticians who began to move away from deduction as *the* way to design sermons to think of themselves as departing from Aristotelian rhetoric. But that, in fact, was not the case; they were simply removing themselves from the dominance of *one* pattern of Aristotle's rhetoric. Much less familiar to homileticians was Aristotle's discussion of the manner and merits of induction.[5] By induction Aristotle meant the use of a series of particular examples to point to a general conclusion. Simply stated, deduction begins with a conclusion, and induction arrives at one. Aristotle found deduction to be more applauded but induction no less persuasive. After all, the carefully selected concrete cases used by induction to build its case move across the hearer's attention like a series of witnesses to the truth espoused. Their cumulative effect is often more telling than a tightly woven syllogism. And induction also has in its favor the fact that it corresponds to the way we experience life and reality, case by case, episode by episode, one particular instance at a time.

Another example of the fruitfulness of a broader reappropriation of rhetoric can be found in the work of Chaim Perelman.[6] Perelman discovered in the classical rhetoricians a principle brought forward by Francis Bacon that is, in brief, "making the absent present." Audiences, says Perelman, attend to that which is present, that which can be seen or heard or felt. A public speaker, however, must often evoke realities that are distant in time or space from the listeners. Vital to the presentation are past and future, but to the audience these are absent. The burden on the speaker is to make the absent present, a task calling for imaginative strategies. Perelman devotes much of *The New Rhetoric* to discussions of the rhetorical methods by which the subject matter becomes present to the audience. What are these methods? Among those urged by Perelman are using singular rather than plural nouns and pronouns; using the present tense in narration, as good newspaper reporters do; having real persons in the presentation rather than simply ideas (a message without a cast of characters seems abstract, unreal); making reference to specific times and places; and incorporating conversation or dialogue rather than giving summary reports of what was said. Recall how much of the Bible consists of direct discourse. The audience listens in and hence feels more present to the event. Although Perelman is not writing homiletics, every preacher who takes seriously the biblical text has felt the burden of making it present for the congregation and welcomes this fresh rereading of ancient rhetoric.

A final gain for preaching from revisiting rhetoric with a broader sense of its contributions is expressed in the now more frequently occurring phrase "rhetoric of excess." The expression first came to me from Frank Kermode and has most recently been developed by Stephen Webb as a form of rhetoric appropriate to theology.[7] The rhetoric of excess has to do with hyperbolic speech, the role of exaggeration in serious discourse. As one would expect, many rhetoricians ancient and modern have found no place for the hyperbole in the treatment of a matter of consequence, regarding it as no more than ornamentation, a concession to "the groundlings" who love such flourishes. All of us have been treated to enough flights of nonsubstantive oratory that we join in resistance to speakers who seek by the high gloss of beautiful exaggerations to blind us to their lack of thought and preparation. Even Isocrates, the rhetorician most associated with the love of eloquence, curbed his own speech and that of his students with the principle of appropriateness to subject matter and occasion. Then should we even look seriously at the rhetoric of excess as a contributor to the preaching of the gospel? The answer is Yes!

Poets and hymn writers have always used hyperbole as not only appropriate but also necessary for the praise of God. The trim, precise, and controlled language of reason alone lacks the size and freedom needed for liturgy. Vocabularies fitted for the boundaries of time and space wait at the foot of the mountain while winged words move ahead. Even theological reflection must come sooner or later to exaggerated speech as an acknowledgment that the subject matter of our discourses—God, creation, providence, redemption, eschatology—is never mastered but bursts beyond the bounds of thought, experience, and language. Consider, for example, the profound theological treatise in Romans 9–11. Paul writes of God's freedom and human freedom, of grace and judgment, of universal salvation and the future of Israel. When Paul has plumbed the depths and ascended the heights of God's purpose for the world, he concludes in the only way appropriate, in a doxological flight beyond his capacity to reason.

> O the depth of the riches and wisdom and knowledge of God!
> How unsearchable are his judgments and how inscrutable his
>   ways!
> "For who has known the mind of the Lord?
> Or who has been his counselor?"
> "Or who has given a gift to him, to receive a gift in return?"
> For from him and through him and to him are all things.
> To him be the glory forever. Amen. (Romans 11:33-36 NRSV)

Transcendence invites hyperbole. If parable is linguistic incarnation, then hyperbole is linguistic transcendence. It is difficult to imagine a sermon that does not press into the service of the gospel the rhetoric of excess. In fact, it is a bit embarrassing that a literary critic (Kermode) and a theologian (Webb) would have to remind the pulpit of its debt to hyperbole.

We began with the question, Is there still room for rhetoric? Implied in the question is a very clear "There *was*" but a very unclear "There *is*." This essay has sought to respond in three ways. First, by recalling how a limited view of rhetoric undergirded the major American homiletical tradition dominating the field for generations, recent reactions against rhetoric become more understandable. Second, by urging caution against a hasty rejection or embrace of rhetoric, we leave a door open for reconsideration. And finally, by reminding ourselves that rhetoric is a field much broader and richer than has been embraced by any single homiletical tradition, an invitation to revisit rhetoric was extended. Even though I am still in the process of accepting that invitation, already I can answer the title question for myself, without hesitation. Yes!

NOTES

1. A homily is a conversation or discussion (Luke 24:14, 15; Acts 20:11) and was an appropriate form for communicating the gospel in small house churches (Acts 20:11; Romans 16:3-5; Philemon 1–2).
2. See the excellent article by Violet Ketels, "Vaclav Havel on Language," *Quinnipac Schweitzer Journal* 1 (1994-95): pp. 19-36.
3. Aristotle *Rhetoric* 1.2.

4. Everyone Familiar with the work of Henry H. Mitchell, especially his *Black Preaching* (Philadelphia and New York: J. B. Lippincott, 1970) and *Celebration and Experience in Preaching* (Nashville: Abingdon Press, 1990), knows his emphasis on preaching that effects change. In a conversation in my home in the spring of 1993, Dr. Mitchell not only reaffirmed this vital purpose but proposed a paper in which he would urge the same on his colleagues in the Academy of Homiletics.
5. See especially Aristotle *Rhetoric* 1.2, 9; 2.20, 25.
6. See especially Chaim Perelman and L. Olbrechts-Tyteca, *The New Rhetoric: A Treatise on Argumentation*, trans. John Wilkinson and Purcell Weaver (South Bend, Ind.: University of Notre Dame Press, 1971).
7. See Robert Alter and Frank Kermode, eds., *The Literary Guide to the Bible* (Cambridge: Harvard University Press, 1987), pp. 387-92; and Stephen Webb, *Blessed Excess* (New York: State University of New York Press, 1993).

CHAPTER SIX

David Buttrick

TEACHING PREACHING IN A NEW CENTURY

*H*ow *does anyone teach preaching? What does it* mean to be a homiletics professor? Ever since Jesus commissioned an unlikely gaggle of disciples, telling them to go into the world with good news, there have been teachers of preaching. In some times and places there is an evangelical urgency to the task. At other times the church seems to back away from the world, and preaching is taught as an in-house activity. But for twenty centuries, disciples have been taught to preach the gospel.

The Eclipse of Homiletics

In our century, professors of homiletics have had a difficult time. For the first quarter of the century, homiletics still commanded a substantial share of the theological curriculum. Often there was a basic course in outlining sermons, followed by intermediate courses in rhetorical elaboration, and then advanced courses on special problems. In addition, there were practice preaching sessions, often monitored by a homiletician in tandem with a teacher of elocution. On top of

75

basic course work, there were electives on preaching biblical texts, preaching doctrinal sermons, evangelistic sermons, sermons for ritual occasions, and so forth. During the early years of the century, theological students probably averaged seven to twelve required semester hours in homiletic study. But in many seminaries lately, homiletics has been reduced to a single introductory course, plus practice preaching sections. There are sometimes a limited number of elective offerings—if the faculty in homiletics has any time to think. These days, with seminaries struggling to survive, schools afford few faculty in the field, sometimes employing a patchwork of local pastors to augment the program. Frequently, there are more faculty in pastoral care or church management than in homiletics. Both fields have been blessed by cultural approval—the "triumph of the therapeutic" and a multiplication of management schools in American universities.[1]

Why did homiletics dwindle in the mid–twentieth century? In part, the field suffered from a necessary collaboration with rhetoric. Once upon a time, rhetoric was part of everyone's required study. After all, rhetoric has been a mainstay of liberal education since the time of Aristotle. Because preaching functions somewhat differently from political or legal oratory, Aristotle's *Poetics* has also been influential.[2] So in every age there have been teachers of preaching who draw on classical rhetoric but, at the same time, are concerned with the peculiarities of declaring the gospel. Ever since Augustine's *De doctrina Christiana*, which embraced classical rhetoric for a Christian purpose,[3] there have been a parade of homiletic books down through the years. Yet in the twentieth century a pall fell on the rhetorical enterprise. Was a technological age impatient with speaking? After all, words did seem impotent beside hydrogen bombs. Or was speaking so corrupted by advertising and politics that the public had begun to speak of "rhetoric" with a sneer?

There is another reason why preaching has been neglected. The rise of an imperialistic biblical theology movement pushed preaching aside. While Karl Barth voiced enthusiasm for preaching and announced that his dogmatics was specifically written for preachers, his definition of preaching tended to scuttle homiletics.[4] He limited preaching to little more than an explanation of the biblical witness—"like the involuntary lip movement of one reading" a scriptural text.[5] Barth did not believe that preachers should engage in conversations with the world's ways of thinking. No, he asserted that the Bible was the word of God and that "the preacher must preach the Bible and nothing else."[6] But Barth's "nothing else" was sweeping and excluded rhetoric, homiletic skills, and any real engagement with culture. Instead of homiletics, students needed only courses in Bible and biblical theology. Rhetoric was rejected as a kind of works righteousness, a striving to make God's word palatable. No, preaching was to speak with no other resource than the Bible's revealed truth. Though Barth declared preaching all important, in the end he devastated the teaching of preaching. By the sixties many mainline seminaries had few students in preaching classes, and religious publishers offered few new works on the subject.

But, please note, preaching was still a calling of God in African American churches. The Black community was nourished by preaching, respected rhetorical tradition, and still admired preachers. Certainly Black congregations were not swept up in the "triumph of the therapeutic." Likewise, because African American preachers read the Bible as story, vision, and promise, they did not tumble into a Barthian biblical positivism.[7] As the homiletic field began to come alive again in the seventies and eighties, works by distinguished African American scholars were significantly involved, most notably, those by Henry H. Mitchell.[8]

Homiletics Revived

All of a sudden, homiletics seems to have recovered. Maybe it has something to do with the number of communication majors crowding college campuses. Or, possibly, homiletics is gaining credence with the application of rhetorical criticism to biblical texts.[9] In theology, there has been an emerging interest in imagination as a locus for theological construction.[10] Thus, homiletics may be on its way "back in" to the center of theological education. In the 1940s pastoral care was renewed by the rise of the psychological sciences; perhaps homiletics will be restored by an enlarging interest in rhetoric.

What should homiletic teaching look like? How can preaching be a pedagogy?[11] At the outset, let us cancel the notion that preachers are born, not taught. Perhaps there are genetic predispositions (who can say?), but some students undoubtedly have had some social advantage.

If a person grows up hearing good preaching, has a lively love of language and an innate feel for rhetorical patterns, such a person will obviously have an edge. African American students' advanced status in homiletics classes has to do, by and large, with two factors: the savvy use of language among ghettoized people, and a genuine respect for preaching in African American communities.[12] Of late, such advantages are denied most White Protestant students. Often they come from middle-class American communities where language is less metaphorically alive[13] and where preaching may have been eroded by the current preoccupation with therapy and church management. But, mark the fact, if preachers can be preshaped, then, obviously, they can be taught.

Can we venture a series of hopes for the teaching of preachers? Here is a tentative list:

1. Homiletics must claim a place in the theological curriculum as a broad concern for the presentation of the gospel.

Obviously, preaching happens both in and outside the church, and happens via words and images.[14] Homiletics must be engaged in understanding the contemporary mind and in thinking how best to present the gospel to our age. In this regard, homiletics will work hand in hand with constructive theology. To use an out-of-date word, as homileticians, we must be teachers of "eristic" theology, a smart sort of missionary theology, in a world where Christians are still a statistical minority.[15] Homiletic teachers must urge students to analyze the culture in which they speak. We can no longer slap down the Bible on a take it or leave it basis; no, we speak in context to a people shaped by context. So homiletics will claim a broad field: How may we speak the gospel to particular people at a particular moment in God's time? Professors of homiletics are not merely "how-to" speech teachers; they are concerned with how the gospel is presented given the culture of our modern age.

2. Homiletics must be concerned with hermeneutics.

Preaching involves interpretation—a double interpreting, for preachers not only unpack texts handed down by tradition but they must "read" the world in which they live.[16] After all, preachers deal in meaning for "a people who walk in darkness." Thus, questions of interpretation are urgent. Ever since critical theory pointed to the problem, we have noticed how social location influences the way in which people read the world and interpret the Bible.[17] White capitalist establishment preachers will not easily grasp texts written by minority peoples. So we must look at contextual hermeneutics.[18] More, we must dare to question the authority of biblical passages. Misunderstood biblical texts have expanded prejudice in our land, not only as texts are shouted by White supremacists, but as texts are used to supress women, condemn Jews, or castigate gay and lesbian persons. Twisted out of shape, the Bible can become a terrible weapon. Bultmann was right: we cannot preach *raw* Scripture; inevitably we "demythologize," explaining the gospel to people within their own thought forms.[19] So homiletic instruction must begin with hermeneutic issues.

3. Homiletics will have to be profoundly spiritual.

I hesitate to use the word *spiritual*, for these days in some circles the term has edged toward implying craziness. But if we do not believe that God is using our speech, indeed speaking redemptively through our stained lips, then preaching will be little more than bad faith and institutional advertising. The African American pulpit rightly has clung to a prophetic definition of preaching. As a result, African American congregations come to church expecting to hear a "Thus saith the Lord" sermon.[20] Meanwhile, most White mainline congregations seem to be reaching for therapy; they crave sermons that will help them manage life successfully. (Such concerns may drift into "buppie" congregations as well.[21])

But the genius of the Protestant tradition is a theology of preaching willing to label sermons "Word of the Lord," not because they begin with the Bible, but because God has chosen ordinary preachers to speak the liberating word.[22] Those who teach preaching must instruct "called" persons, and instill in students both Isaiah's awe—"I am a man of unclean lips" (Isa. 6:5 NRSV)—and Jeremiah's passion—"If I say, 'I will not . . . speak' . . . there is something like a burning fire shut up in my bones" (Jer. 20:9 NRSV). Preaching must be redemptive and prophetic at the same time. Thus preaching ought to happen in the midst of a praying preacher's lifelong conversation with God.

4. Homiletics must be technically demanding.

Public speaking is not "natural"; it has to be learned. But what do we learn? Older homiletic textbooks no longer seem true.[23] In our century, every language in the world has traded one vocabulary for another. When dictionaries have to be rewritten, along with Bibles and prayer books, then a whole wide world is busy changing its mind. We live in the midst of a cultural revolution as radical as the collapse of the Greco-Roman world or the dissolution of the Medieval synthesis. Preaching in the future will address a very different world than our now fading "Protestant Era."[24] As a result we will have to discover anew how to address listeners with the gospel. Homileticians will join rhetoricians in researching a whole new repertoire of "how-to" speaker's wisdom. For such a task, the African American community is crucial. African American churches have kept rhetorical concern, a tradition of speakers' "know-how" that needs to be shared.

5. Homiletics must renew a proper alliance with theology.

During the rise and fall of the biblical theology movement, a period roughly from 1930 through 1980,[25] homiletics was taught as "preaching the Bible." Electives in most seminaries featured courses on how to preach from different books of the Bible, particularly Gospel readings from a lectionary cycle. But preaching is not limited to the Bible page alone. The gospel message must be preached in a contemporary way to contemporary people as liberating good news—whether found on a page of the Bible or simply recalled in the context of Christian praise. We must beware of a restrictive, limiting biblicism that can too easily turn into law, stifling the Spirit. In preaching, our task is always theological. We are expressing the meaning of the gospel for people in location, that is, in a place at a time and with a particular cultural mind. Thus, preaching along with theology is ever rethinking the gospel and respeaking God's good news in new ways.[26]

6. Homiletics must be taught as an evangelical concern.

Lately there are voices urging the church to be separate from the world, particularly from our modern secular world. We are told to preserve our identity as God's own special people.[27] Such a concern is attractive not only to eroded White Protestant churches that have been losing membership, but also to African American churches that, since the time of the Civil War, have had to hold on tight in order to survive in a racist society. But separation is perilous for preaching. We are under the evangelical mandate of the resurrection angels; we must "go tell." Though we tend to label the secular world our "enemy," in spite of its corruption, sinfulness, and perversion, the world is still defined by John 3:16, namely, as a world God loves. Remember, our Lord warned that those who would save their lives will lose them. For the sake of God we must risk ourselves evangelically, preaching to those who have become strangers to the gospel, whether in protected White suburbs or in streetwise city enclaves, in gutted housing projects or along the carpeted corridors of corporate power. Today's secular generation is breeding a people who will not know the good news; once more, homiletics may become a missionary strategy here in our own land.

Homiletics is a difficult field. The so-called "academic disciplines" regard homiletics as an unacademic how-to enterprise, even though the first advanced seminar in theological fields was in homiletics.[28] So homiletic teachers will have to be bright, sweepingly learned, and willing to converse intelligently with other theological disciplines. Homileticians should be the best-read persons on any faculty. They are dedicated to finding out how to speak the gospel, and thus have a special perspective to share with other disciplines. What is it like to teach preaching? Well, we preach, teach, think, and study more fields at once than most human beings. But we do so with the sweet laughter of those who live in grace, leaving the outcome of our profession in God's good hands.

NOTES

1. Philip Rieff's *The Triumph of the Therapeutic: Uses of Faith After Freud* (New York: Harper & Row, 1966) was prescient. Thirty years ago, Rieff predicted the rise of psychoanalytic perspectives displacing theological meaning. And Edward Farley suggests that "the therapeutic and the managerial [have] become, then, the framework of contemporary clergy hermeneutics." See "Praxis and Piety: Hermeneutics Beyond the New Dualism," in *Justice and the Holy: Essays in Honor of Walter Harrelson*, ed. Douglas A. Knight and Peter J. Paris (Atlanta: Scholars Press, 1989), p. 247.
2. For a recent translation, see Aristotle, *Poetics*, trans. S. H. Butcher (New York: Hill and Wang, 1961), with a very helpful introduction by Francis Fergusson; also see Artistole, *On Rhetoric: A Theory of Civic Discourse*, trans. George A. Kennedy (New York: Oxford University Press, 1991).

3. Augustine, *On Christian Doctrine*, trans. D. W. Robertson Jr. (New York: Bobbs-Merrill, 1958). See also Eugene TeSelle, *Augustine's Strategy As an Apologist* (Philadelphia: Villanova University Press, 1974).

4. For example, see Karl Barth, *The Göttingen Dogmatics: Instruction in the Christian Religion*, vol. 1, ed. H. Reifflen, trans. G. W. Bromiley (Grand Rapids, Mich.: William B. Eerdmans, 1991), pp. 14-68.

5. Karl Barth, *Homiletics*, trans. Geoffrey W. Bromiley and Donald E. Daniels (Louisville, Ky.: Westminster/John Knox, 1991), p. 76.

6. Karl Barth, *The Preaching of the Gospel*, trans. B. E. Hooke (Philadelphia: Westminster Press, 1963), p. 43.

7. I have so argued in "Preaching, Hermeneutics, and Liberation," in *Standing with the Poor*, ed. Paul P. Parker (Cleveland: Pilgrim Press, 1992), pp. 95-107.

8. Henry H. Mitchell has written much that has been seminal. His early studies were particularly influential for the renewal of homiletics: *Black Preaching* (Philadelphia and New York: J. B. Lippincott, 1970); *The Recovery of Preaching* (San Francisco: Harper & Row, 1977); and, more recently, *Celebration and Experience in Preaching* (Nashville: Abingdon Press, 1990).

9. For example, see George A. Kennedy, *New Testament Interpretation Through Rhetorical Criticism* (Chapel Hill: The University of North Carolina Press, 1984); and Burton L. Mack, *Rhetoric and the New Testament* (Minneapolis: Fortress Press, 1990), with a helpful bibliography.

10. For example, see Gordon D. Kaufman, *In the Face of Mystery: A Constructive Theology* (Cambridge: Harvard University Press, 1993), ch. 3; as well as *Essay on Theological Method* (Atlanta: Scholars Press, 1979); and *The Theological Imagination: Constructing the Concept of God* (Philadelphia: Westminster Press, 1985). For a somewhat more conservative treatment, Garrett Green, *Imagining God: Theology and the Religious Imagination* (San Francisco: Harper & Row, 1989).

11. See Don M. Wardlaw, ed., *Learning Preaching: Understanding and Participating in the Process* (Lincoln, Ill.: The Academy of Homiletics, 1989).

12. For example, see "The 15 Greatest Black Preachers," *Ebony* 49, no. 1 (November 1993): pp. 156-68.

13. For a study of "block language," see Philip E. Wheelwright, *Metaphor and Reality* (Bloomington: Indiana University Press, 1962).

14. Kathy Black has rightly raised the issue of preaching for the deaf through "signing." See her "Beyond the Spoken Word: Preaching As Presence," in *The Academy of Homiletics: Papers of the Annual Meeting* (Washington, D.C.: December 1993), pp. 79-88.

15. On "eristics theology," see Emil Brunner, *The Christian Doctrine of God*, trans. Olice Wyon (Philadelphia: Westminster Press, 1950), pp. 98-103.

16. See Edward Farley, "Interpreting Situations: An Inquiry into the Nature of Practical Theology," in *Formation and Reflection: The Promise of Practical Theology*, ed. L. S. Mudge and J. N. Poling (Philadelphia: Fortress Press, 1987), pp. 1-26.

17. See David Held, *Introduction to Critical Theory: Horkheimer to Habermas* (Berkeley: University of California Press, 1980).

18. Henry H. Mitchell has recognized hermeneutic context. In particular, see *Black Belief: Folk Beliefs of Blacks in America and West Africa* (New York: Harper & Row, 1975); *Black Preaching: the Recovery of a Powerful Art* (Nashville: Abingdon Press, 1990); and with Nicholas C. Cooper-Lewter, *Soul Theology: The Heart of American Black Culture* (San Francisco: Harper & Row, 1986; reprint, Nashville: Abingdon Press, 1991).

19. Rudolf Bultmann, *Jesus Christ and Mythology* (New York: Charles Scribner's Sons, 1958).

20. So argues William B. McClain, in *Come Sunday, The Liturgy of Zion* (Nashville: Abingdon Press, 1990), p. 70.

21. Cornel West, in *Keeping Faith: Philosophy and Race in America* (New York: Routledge, 1993), is not sanguine about what he terms the role of the "black, petite bourgeoisie," pp. 74-77, 287-90. See also the sermons in Henry H. Mitchell and Emil M. Thomas, *Preaching for Black Self-Esteem* (Nashville: Abingdon Press, 1994), ch. 7.

22. See my book, *A Captive Voice: The Liberation of Preaching* (Louisville, Ky.: Wesminster/John Knox, 1994), pp. 21-28, 38-43.
23. In research conducted over the past twenty years, we have been astonished to discover that much of the practical rhetorical advice in older homiletics texts (e.g. Andrew W. Blackwood, *The Preparation of Sermons* [Nashville: Abingdon Press, 1948] or Ilion T. Jones, *Principles and Practice of Preaching: A Comprehensive Study of the Art of Sermon Construction* (Nashville: Abingdon Press, 1956]) is no longer useful. Apparently human consciousness has changed. See discussions in my *Homiletic* (Philadelphia: Fortress Press, 1987), pt. 1; and also *A Captive Voice: The Liberation of Preaching* (Louisville, Ky.: Westminster/John Knox, 1994), ch. 4.
24. The term is borrowed from Paul Tillich, (*The Protestant Era*, trans. James Luther Adams [The University of Chicago Press, 1948]), and refers to the epoch beginning with the Renaissance and Reformation and ending in the middle of the twentieth century.
25. See Brevard S. Childs, *Biblical Theology in Crisis* (Philadelphia: Westminster Press, 1970), pt. 1.
26. For example, American preaching has described salvation in personal, inward terms. How will we describe salvation in interpersonal terms? The task must be worked out practically in pulpits as well as in theological tomes. See Edward Farley, *Good and Evil: Interpreting a Human Condition* (Minneapolis: Fortress Press, 1990), chs. 1–3.
27. A theme articulated in Stanley Hauerwas and William H. Willimon, *Resident Aliens: Life in the Christian Colony* (Nashville: Abingdon Press, 1989).
28. An alert theologian-homiletician, Quinn Fox has provided the information: Late in the eighteenth century, perhaps under the impact of both Kant and Schleiermacher, the University of Göttingen established an advanced *Predigerseminar*, prior to inaugurating similar seminars in theology. See Charles A. Briggs, *History of the Study of Theology*, vol. 2, prepared for publication by Emilie G. Briggs (London: Duckworth, 1916), pp. 18, 182-83.

CHAPTER SEVEN

Paul Scott Wilson

D O C T R I N E   I N

P R E A C H I N G :   H A S

I T   A   F U T U R E ?

*Earlier in this century, to consider the future of doc-*trine in preaching as though there could have been any question of its role might have seemed surprising. Doctrine comprises the teachings of the church that are the core of its self-understanding and life. Doctrine centers on Jesus Christ. It is an expression of the communal life of the church as it seeks to understand its faith convictions, whether by proposition, example, analogy, parable, paradigm, metaphor, or question.[1] Like strands of one rope, doctrine, preaching, and theology braid a lifeline through history.

Even as our understanding of teaching has widened in recent decades, a narrower use of the word *doctrine* has become common: the explicit formal propositional teachings of the church.[2] Doctrine becomes suspect for good reasons: throughout history Christians have mistakenly reduced narrative to propositional claims;[3] misuse of authority and power in church and society is painfully clear; and society tends to disclaim the possibility of objective truth. Forms of expression such as story, metaphor, and image seem more conducive to communicating experience and inviting participation. Some people are persuaded of the adequacy of postmodern language theory for the Christian enterprise. In this, language has no objective external referent outside of itself, and even the biblical text has no meaning apart from what the reader brings to it.[4] Preachers and theologians, experiencing the divisiveness of some doctrines, can find themselves caving in to relativism and utter deconstruction at a time when many people in the pews are without church backgrounds and are in need of Christian instruction.

We are not talking about those lax preachers who in every age have been all too willing to jettison theology and have tossed out ropes from the church that were either too short to reach those who were sinking or so frayed and raveled that they would break before the needy found firm footing. Rather, we are concerned with responsible preachers who would not seek to dispense with theology. They seek an alternative to propositional or doctrinal formulation. Fortunately, there are more choices available to the inquiring preacher than the simple rejection of propositional doctrine.

It is appropriate to explore these alternatives in a volume dedicated to Henry H. Mitchell. Many, though not all, of the alternatives to doctrine in preaching we will cite are anticipated by Mitchell and his tradition. First with fire in 1970 (*Black Preaching*), and with continued passion and insight into the present, he has made available to preachers around the world homiletical understandings from arguably the richest preaching tradition today. This tradition arises out of a culture that knows oppression, a culture in which doctrine can never be long separated from a vital God concerned with the spiritual and social needs of people.

We may categorize doctrinal options in four related groups: *liberation theology, narrative theology, postliberal theology as represented by George Lindbeck*, and *rhetoric*. Each of these offers legitimate possibilities for preachers. The latter two have received the least explicit homiletical attention and will receive the most space here. In our age, all of these alternatives seem to focus on experience. Yet it is what key doctrines refer to, not the experience they reflect, that is of ultimate importance. With so much recent attention to what our doctrines say about us (our biases and privileges), we can fail to hear what God is saying through them—who God is and who we are in relationship to God.

(1) Liberation Theology. Every age must reexamine its doctrines in light of Scripture and experience. Liberation, Black, feminist, and womanist theologians have dramatically changed major doctrines. There are reasons to challenge doctrines such as the Whiteness of God, which perpetuates the biases of dominant Western culture;[5] the maleness of God and Christ, which perpetuates male as the Christian norm for relationships, ethics, and ministry;[6] the redemptive nature of suffering, which justifies suffering and can be an affront to those who have been abused;[7] and sin as pride and rebellion, which disregards the sin of lack of pride, lack of ambition, and absence of power.[8] These shifts have had a major impact on the pulpit, particularly on hermeneutical approaches to the text and to doctrines.

(2) Narrative Theology. Narrative alternatives to doctrine have been said to (a) retain the narrative import of much of Scripture,[9] (b) provide a more adequate reflection of human experience,[10] and (c) enlist the individual in the moral vision and action of the larger Christian story.[11] Homileticians like Henry Mitchell, Edmund Steimle, Charles Rice, and Fred Craddock helped initiate and perpetuate this discussion. They advocated the need for recovery of scriptural stories for the pulpit, for sermons to lead toward concretion rather than abstraction, for the preacher to reflect congregational life experience, for story that makes its own point, and for sermons to be structured in ways other than deductive propositional fashion. This has meant increased attention to poetics—the principles of form, plot, character, emotion, and the like, which govern art and literature.

(3) Postliberal Theology. George A. Lindbeck's 1984 proposal continues to receive discussion and deserves homiletical attention. He sought less to recast or restructure propositional doctrine than to reconceive its function within the community. His postliberal approach to doctrine is theoretical and hypothetical, and arose out of ecumenical discussions. Perhaps it was not intended for homiletical application or testing, and will receive its true test, as he claims, in the future, when Christians from diverse perspectives might have greater need for conversation and cooperation. In spite of this untested potential, his cultural-linguistic approach to doctrine holds intriguing preaching possibilities.

Lindbeck dismisses traditional "cognitive-propositional" theories of doctrine that pretend to make truth claims about objective realities:

using them, doctrinal agreement can only be reached "if one or both sides abandon their earlier positions."[12] He also dismisses "experiential-expressive" liberal theories of doctrine, which began with Schleiermacher, and which imply universal, culturally independent responses to religious feelings and experience. Doctrines in this mode function as nondiscursive symbols whose meanings are various, and thus cannot command precise conformity or agreement. Lindbeck favors what he calls a postliberal "cultural-linguistic" theory that views doctrine as "regulative," or as "rules," much in the manner that a normative lexicon and grammar in language allow us to speak in meaningful ways.[13] He believes his theory allows for the cognitive and experiential, as well as for cultural differences.

Lindbeck's noble goal was to find a means for reconciliation of doctrinal differences without "capitulation" by one or another party. Ecumenical dialogue achieves this, he says, by specifying when each rule might apply or by stipulating when one takes precedence. Tradition is handed on through a community's adoption of the narratives of Jesus Christ and by values passed down through history. Consistency is found within the Christian "language" as a whole, rather than in specific formulations, symbols, or religious experiences that may vary from person to person or culture to culture (in the same manner that two English-speaking people are able to communicate meaningfully, though they might not share precisely the same vocabulary, dialect, or accent).

His cultural-linguistic option offers attractive possibilities for the preacher. First, many of today's congregations are composed of people with diverse doctrinal understandings and backgrounds from within and outside the Christian tradition. There is remarkable scholarly consensus today that biblical texts must provide the narrative base for the community. Lindbeck argues that Christians must dwell imaginatively in those texts: he holds Henry Mitchell's understanding of this as a model.[14] Where individuals are tempted to divide on the basis of doctrinal difference, there can be, at minimum, agreement on the basic story, and to some measure even on its interpretation.

Second, a cultural-linguistic doctrine paradigm implies genuine community—not just of like-minded people with similar experience. Christ speaks to faithful people in different ways and at different stages in moral and spiritual growth and discernment. If the preacher rhetorically anticipates appropriate diversity, and values rather than fears it, then the sermon can better assist God's purpose of bestowing genuine community.

Third, in such a model, doctrinal affirmation arises more out of the story of common life and mission than out of intellectual assent detached from participation. Mitchell would add that the intellectual or rational dimension of our faith cannot be separated from our intuitive, emotional, or experiential dimensions.[15] To make determinations about someone's character on the basis of how he or she formulates ideas or whether those ideas agree with one's own can be a grave mistake. To experience how that person exercises ministry may also be needed. In other words, doctrine becomes less an item to be examined in a Christian legal display case, and is increasingly something that is lived.

In spite of its strengths, there are problems with a cultural-linguistic approach to doctrine for the pulpit. First, while this approach tries to embrace diversity, it in fact implies a greater uniformity and will for cooperation than may generally exist. In any congregation there are a range of understandings about the interpretation, role, centrality, and necessity of particular doctrines. Individual members have attitudes toward doctrine that may resemble one or more of Lindbeck's three perspectives. Reconceiving the function of doctrine does not avoid "capitulation": it is still required, for instance, in the mission life of a congregation when controversial issues are argued theologically. For instance, opening a church to the homeless might mean alienating many of the church's neighbors and members. Theological arguments concerning the doctrine of ministry may be available on both sides, but yes or no decides the case. One must choose.

Second, Lindbeck prescribes a unity that need not exist. All doctrines need not be valued equally and rarely are. There are some fundamental doctrines, concerning creation, incarnation, Christ, and the church, for instance, that are legitimately understood in cognitive-propositional ways. They impart certain timeless truths discerned through faith, however inadequate our words may be. In fact, preachers are always needing to focus on central doctrines of the faith, essential doctrines that help to sustain believers and define the community of faith and mission.

Third, Lindbeck implies that the heart of religious tradition lies in its historical ideas and values, as though doctrines do not have an external referent, and do not point beyond themselves to the reality of a relationship with God. Many of our doctrines (and sermons) function as both a means of revelation and as appropriate conceptual truth. Sermons that do not focus on God and on the reality of God's action end up being sermons in which listeners strain to hear God. Preachers name and claim God's action in the world, as well as the meaning of that action, often in propositional ways that assist the reception of the message. Yet as James Wm. McClendon Jr. notes, "such propositional doctrines are not the only or even the chief means of doctrinal teaching."[16]

Finally, Lindbeck's dismissal of the experiential-expressive theory is too swift. Doctrines in this theory function as nondiscursive symbols. As such, they may well lack precision for agreement, yet this ambiguity in itself can be a source that permits agreement without capitulation. The preacher need not expound the means of Jesus' resurrection from the dead to assert the facts and their meaning. The biblical accounts already function for some people as symbols, for others as literal stories, and for others in other ways, perhaps not fully conceptualized, explored, or articulated. The ambiguity inherent in communal reception of the doctrine is less important than the fact to which we attest, that the risen Christ has confronted us in our lives with saving power.

By contrast, Lindbeck seems to deny the possibility of common experience, in diverse locations and cultures, of the risen Christ, and of common expression and understanding of that experience. Emil Brunner spoke of the event dimension of revelation in *Truth as Encounter*.[17] Were Lindbeck correct, there would be no point in appealing to experience in preaching. But preachers should use the widest range of communication tools, including doctrinal reflection on experience, whenever they seek to bring people into an encounter with Jesus Christ. The truth of the matter is that God chooses to use these various means to speak the Word that is God's way of salvation.

(4) Rhetoric. We have been considering alternatives for treating doctrine in the pulpit. In addition to revising doctrine, or to restructuring it as narrative, or to reconceiving the function of doctrine as rule, there is a fourth alternative to which we are attentive. Doctrine has important differences and similarities with rhetoric, the classical means of determining what will be persuasive in an argument or discourse. Rhetoric extends much beyond doctrine to all matters of effective communication. Nonetheless, doctrine can be conceived in part as rhetoric, as a tool of persuasion—or as a tool of identification, to employ Kenneth Burke's emphasis in contemporary rhetoric.[18]

In other words, while doctrine imparts certain truths, or experiences, or rules, it also is a means of discourse or conversation that can enable the community we seek. Relationships are facilitated by doctrine, particularly the congregation's (and the preacher's) relationship with God, who chooses to be met through the proclamation of the Word. The preacher strives to use words in a manner that most readily assists what God is graciously trying to accomplish through the sermon; thus in Mitchell's tradition, the preacher moves people to celebration and experience.[19] In the same tradition, preachers like Charles G. Adams use rhythmic structuring of doctrinal passages to enable emotional and intellectual communication.[20]

When doctrine is conceived as a tool of rhetorical persuasion, it again can be understood not as rigid and static truth that must be accepted as a package—although doctrinal truth has a universal or eternal dimension—but as a means of pointing to truth, of inviting people into their own faithful relationship with God. God actively uses such proclamation to persuade the seeking listener, to bring that person to a profession of truth through faithful dialogue within Christian communion. Doctrine, in this mode, is conversation inviting response, witness inviting participation, testimony to experience that seeks a meeting of God in and through experiences. Our words will always be inadequate. Doctrine is thus a means of faith seeking understanding that trusts God to work in relationships that constitute the church.

Karl Barth helped preachers to recover a vital understanding of God at work in the sermon. He also tried to ensure the demise of any focus on rhetoric in preaching,[21] in spite of Augustine's influential work in this regard. The comeback of rhetoric in homiletics since Barth has been gradual, and until the last decade, largely through the back door, without use of the word *rhetoric*,[22] which had so many negative connotations. The recovery of rhetoric in education, as well as the influence of strong rhetorical traditions, like the oral African American one in preaching, have led the way. Rhetorical concern with meeting the needs of the listener and involving the listener in the act of communication helps to mark the current revolution in homiletics.

This is a time of great need in the Christian church. In seeking more effective ways of communicating the gospel, we cannot ignore rhetoric, as voices in many new volumes on preaching are now saying. By the same token, we cannot afford to advocate or practice simplistic choices that would do away with propositional doctrine in preaching. Rather, preachers need to consider a full range of options that include, at the least, the following: revising propositions; restructuring doctrines as narratives; reconceiving the function of doctrine as language; and reclaiming doctrine as rhetoric. Perhaps with a clearer understanding of available options, the rope of faith that we place in others' hands may be found well-braided, less frayed, and taut with God's grace.

N O T E S

1. This understanding has been helpfully explored in William J. Carl III, *Preaching Christian Doctrine* (Philadelphia: Fortress Press, 1984), pp. 5-9.
2. The separation of theology and doctrine is a necessary presupposition for George A. Lindbeck in his positing a cultural-linguistic approach to religion in his *The Nature of Doctrine: Religion and Theology in a Postliberal Age* (Philadelphia: Westminster Press, 1984), pp. 76-77.
3. Hans Frei, *The Eclipse of the Biblical Narrative: A Study in Eighteenth- and Nineteenth-Century Hermeneutics* (New Haven: Yale University Press, 1974). On a related matter, David Greenshaw has noted, "The specific failing [of the biblical theology movement] lay not in the search for concepts as such but in the more fundamental presumption that concepts lay behind what was said [in Scripture]" (David Greenshaw, "As One with Authority," in *Intersection: Post-Critical Studies in Preaching*, ed. Richard L. Eslinger [Grand Rapids, Mich.: William B. Eerdmans, 1994], p. 111).
4. See Stanley Hauerwas's uncritical adoption of Stanley Fish in *Unleashing the Scripture: Freeing the Bible from Captivity to America* (Nashville: Abingdon Press, 1993), pp. 19-28. See also my paper dealing with contemporary language theory, "Postmodernism, Theology and Preaching," in *Papers of the Annual Meeting of the Academy of Homiletics*, Durham, N.C., 1994, pp. 149-58.
5. See James Cone, *A Black Theology of Liberation* (Maryknoll, N.Y.: Orbis, 1990 [1986], esp. p. 63.
6. See Rosemary R. Ruether, *Sexism and God-Talk: Toward a Feminist Theology* (Boston: Beacon Press, 1983); and Katie G. Cannon, *Black Womanist Ethics* (Atlanta: Scholars Press, 1988).
7. See Joanne Carlson Brown and Carole R. Bohn, eds., *Christianity, Patriarchy and Abuse: A Feminist Critique* (New York: Pilgrim Press, 1989).
8. See Judith Plaskow, *Sex, Sin and Grace: Women's Experience and the Theologies of Reinhold Niebuhr and Paul Tillich* (Lanham, Md.: University Press of America, 1980).
9. Hans Frei's work was anticipated by works such as Amos N. Wilder, *Early Christian Rhetoric: The Language of the Gospel* (Cambridge: Harvard University Press, 1971).
10. The classic essay on this is Stephen Crites, "The Narrative Quality of Experience," in *Why Narrative?: Readings in Narrative Theology*, eds. Stanley Hauerwas and L. Gregory Jones (Grand Rapids, Mich.: William B. Eerdmans, 1989).

11. Stanley Hauerwas, *A Community of Character: Toward a Constructive Christian Social Ethic* (South Bend, Ind.: University of Notre Dame Press, 1981).
12. Lindbeck, *The Nature of Christian Doctrine*, p. 17.
13. Lindbeck, *The Nature of Christian Doctrine*, pp. 16-19, 82.
14. George A. Lindbeck, "The Church's Mission to a Postmodern Culture," in *Postmodern Theology: Christian Faith in a Postmodern World*, Frederic B. Burnham, ed. (San Francisco: Harper, 1989), pp. 37-55, especially p. 42.
15. Henry H. Mitchell, *Celebration and Experience in Preaching* (Nashville: Abingdon Press, 1990), pp. 21-23.
16. James Wm. McClendon Jr., *Systematic Theology: Doctrine*, vol. 2. (Nashville: Abingdon Press, 1994), p. 30. See his good discussion of Lindbeck on pp. 30-32.
17. Emil Brunner, *Truth as Encounter* (Philadelphia: Westminster Press, 1964).
18. See Craig A. Lascalzo's discussion of Burke in "A Rhetorical Model," in *Hermeneutics for Preaching: Approaches to Contemporary Interpretation of Scripture*, ed. Raymond Bailey (Broadman, 1993), pp. 105-34; and in his *Preaching Sermons that Connect: Effective Communication Through Identification* (Downer's Grove, Ill.: InterVarsity Press, 1992).
19. Henry H. Mitchell, *Celebration and Experience in Preaching* (Nashville: Abingdon Press, 1990), especially pp. 61-76.
20. I have discussed Adams in my *The Practice of Preaching* (Nashville: Abingdon Press, 1995) p. 56. See Also Henry Mitchell's discussion of rhythm and related matters in his *Black Preaching: The Recovery of a Powerful Art* (Nashville: Abingdon Press, 1990), especially p. 91.

21. See Thomas G. Long's discussion of Barth and Brunner in "And How Shall They Hear? The Listener in Contemporary Preaching," in *Listening to the Word: Studies in Honor of Fred B. Craddock*, eds. Gail R. O'Day and Thomas G. Long (Nashville: Abingdon Press, 1993), pp. 167-88; especially pp. 174-80.
22. Generally, on the rare occasions when the word *rhetoric* did appear, it was in relation to the history of preaching. This was the case with William J. Carl III, who devoted a section to the rhetoric of Augustine and David H. C. Read in *Preaching Christian Doctrine*, pp. 104-12.

CHAPTER EIGHT

James Earl Massey

THE PREACHER
WHO WOULD BE
A TEACHER

*T*he church began under the ministry of an itinerant teaching preacher known as Jesus of Nazareth. Those who heard him teach called him "Rabbi" because of his masterful style and the engaging substance of his work. The Aramaic *rabbi,* "my master," was the title of address used when conversing with Jewish teachers of repute. It is used again and again in the Gospel accounts when persons address Jesus as he teaches.[1] The New Testament writings reflect the fact that the spirit of teaching was strong in the churches during the first century. Two reasons stood behind this: (1) Jesus had been "a teacher who has come from God" (John 3:2), which made the teaching ministry stand in continuing esteem; and (2) the church leaders Jesus appointed to continue his ministry knew that sound living depends upon sound teaching.[2]

The early teachers of the church planned strategically, intent to guide the awakened intellect, provide religious answers for the questioning mind, and offer a systematized body of truths for the questing soul. The teaching reflected and reported in the New Testament writings mainly involves "believers," persons already won to the Christian faith through the preaching of the gospel. The Epistles show that *didache* (what is taught) was understood as necessary follow-up to *kerygma* (what is proclaimed), although a complete distinction between these cannot always be seen in the literature.[3] By the time the Pastoral Epistles were written, it was expected that one who chose to be a pastor would also be "an apt teacher" (1 Tim. 3:2). In fact, the stipulations regarding pastoral ministry made teaching an imperative function.[4]

Across the ages, the church has always needed and expected a teaching ministry.[5] Henry Sloan Coffin writes:

> The prophetic office of the Christian preacher has been grossly exaggerated. A preacher may prophesy on occasion; but Elijah, Amos and Hosea, Isaiah, Jeremiah and Ezekiel were not parish ministers. None of them preached statedly to the same congregations; most of them handled a very few aspects of truth. A Greater than they was usually called Teacher, and it would be wiser for Christian preachers to strive to be worthy of that title.... A preacher who would minister in the same pulpit for a quarter of a century, or for at least a decade, and would train a congregation in convictions and ideals, in methods of intercourse with the Unseen in ways of serving the commonweal must follow a similar educational system.[6]

I

Given the unique history and posture of American society, no professional role has been more strategic to social progress than that of the teaching pastor. The founding and continuing development of the nation's churches, together with their strategic impact upon the development of the character of the nation during this experiment in democracy, has depended in great measure upon the work of teaching pastors.[7]

As servant-leader in a church, the pastor shares status and authority with all others called and commissioned to be "trust officers" in the service of the Lord. Called and sent to share and pass on the kerygmatic message about salvation, and to train believers in the values and implementation of the good news from God, the pastor is expected to teach what the church teaches. In this service, he or she follows the lead of the first Christian preachers and teachers, aptly described by

Albert C. Outler as "traditioners—trust officers of the Christian treasure of truth, qualified judges of 'right teaching.' "[8] As a teacher, the pastor not only identifies that tradition but is identified with it and by it.

The Christian gospel is God's invitation to an experience, an experience inclusive of moral, spiritual, and social effects. The New Testament literature is the initial record of that experience as registered in the lives of distinct persons, and that record is the main sourcebook for the noble, serious, instructive, and necessary work of the teaching pastor. It is from within the province of this distinct biblical record that the Christian preacher is expected and authorized to teach what the church teaches.

In addition to teaching what the universal church teaches, however, the preacher is also expected to inspire and promote by teaching what generates social uplift and human advancement through freedom, justice, fairness, and the steady pursuit of community.

When the scriptural message is rightly understood and applied, it should be obvious that such benefits of social uplift and human advancement are really ends sought by biblical faith. Failure to grasp the fuller implications of the gospel for the whole of life can only lead to a bifurcation between the soul's needs and one's other, more material needs. Although some religious teachers have been faulted for over-emphasizing the biblical tradition's compensatory and otherworldly elements, it must not be overlooked that the social accommodation nurtured by such an emphasis has usually been related to some social crisis that seemed unyielding.[9]

It should also be understood that the very emphasis upon uplifting must lead to thought and action about changing social conditions for the better. The failure to recognize this dialectical interplay between accommodation and strategic achievement hinders due appreciation for what preachers must be about as servant-educators among the people. It also hinders one from seeing justice as defined by those on the bottom, and hinders one from seeing that American society is thoroughly entrenched in racism.

Linked by calling and tradition to the event and message of Jesus Christ, the pastor is expected to be a servant of God's Word to the world. Teaching what the church teaches, he or she shares in that grand succession of those who proclaim, interpret, and seek to fulfill the

Christian faith. Linked by life and experience with people struggling to survive and achieve in a secularistic and otherwise problematic society, the pastor is expected to apply the insights of the faith for the encouragement, uplift, and guidance of the people.

II

There are at least four strategic means by which the ordained minister may teach. First, there is the "*mass appeal*" *of preaching*. Preaching allows moral and spiritual instruction to be shared in mass fashion, in a popular medium, but with individual impact.

According to the Synoptic Gospels, there was an evident blend between preaching and teaching in the spoken words of Jesus. There are passages in the Gospel accounts in which the terms *preaching* and *teaching* are used interchangeably, so that the action of Jesus in addressing his hearers in public appears pointedly didactic and declarative at the same time. Jesus instructed in order to inspire; he had to give content in order to share comfort. Understanding is imperative for those who seek to live out their faith, and aptness in relating biblical truths to personal questions and needs of people keeps the teaching preacher linked with them as an essential helper of their faith. The readiness and skill to instruct must surely be reflected when the congregation gathers to worship God and be addressed out of God's Word.

True religious experience is more than an emotional mood; it is a vital happening in response to something taught and caught. The climate of modernity does not inspire faith, but it does press persons to seek and locate a faith. Preaching calls attention to the Christian faith, and it does so by isolating certain facts and truths from inside the experience of that faith. Preaching that is religiously instructive will naturally be doctrinal. Charles Spurgeon is reported to have said that "The most fervent revivalism will wear itself out in mere smoke, if it be not maintained by the fuel of teaching."[10]

A concern to share doctrine must be part of the preacher's passion—not doctrine for doctrine's sake but for the sake of the people's understanding and use of faith to live. In order to focus the use of doctrine, the preacher must first understand the way doctrine can help those he or she is preaching to. Doctrine then breathes life; it shows itself as more than an abstract subject and claims attention as a necessary message that attracts, alerts, and assures. The earnest preacher seeks to make the most correct statement of the truth with which he or she is dealing, but that statement must be pertinent to the sensed needs of those who are to hear it. Biblical doctrines matter for life at its best. They satisfy the soul's quest for truth, and they liberate the mind by engaging the thoughts. The preaching that really matters does not separate inspiration from something taught.

Howard Thurman writes about how impressed his grandmother was with the preaching that she, a former slave, had heard from a certain slave preacher when she was a girl. That slave preacher had drilled into the consciousness of his Black hearers the notion that they did not have to feel inferior because they were enslaved. Thurman writes, "How everything in me quivered with the pulsing tremor of raw energy when, in her recital, she would come to the triumphant climax of the minister: 'You are not niggers. You—you are not slaves. You are God's children.' This established for them the ground of personal dignity."[11] And out of that profound sense of being children of God, those slaves could handle the pressures of their days. The idea that they were children of God was a shared idea, a focused teaching for which that slave preacher felt responsible while addressing his fellow slaves. How different his teaching, both in spirit and substance, from that of the White preacher who occasionally addressed them, but always about being "obedient to them that are your masters . . . as unto Christ" (Eph. 6:5 KJV).[12] The White preacher who served the master's interests argued his doctrine defensively, intent to keep the slaves submissive; the slave preacher applied his doctrine in the interests of his hearers, intent to liberate their spirits. This is the true function of sound teaching.

A second means by which the pastor teaches is by *counseling*. Pastoral counseling ranks among the central services a pastor is expected to make available to those who seek it. The pastor's effectiveness in counseling will depend upon many factors, of course, but the ability and readiness to share insights and perspectives with persons who need help cannot be overemphasized.

Wayne E. Oates has listed several levels within the field or service of pastoral care, and one of those levels is that of teaching.[13] As an interpreter of the Scriptures, as an ordained servant of the church, the pastor's perspectives are viewed more often than not as of instructional value. The necessity to instruct seems clear when dealing with persons whose moral and religious views are problematic, or whose attitudes are unhealthy, or whose experiences need clarifying conversation. The religious care of troubled persons includes the need to share information and insights as well as the need to provide a caring presence.

The pastor's counsel will be given to share insights, rehearse meanings, answer questions, resolve conflicts, appeal to motives, heal inward injuries, stimulate faith, purge the soul, promote change, provide emotional release, encourage persons to venture, and grant enablement. Rightly done, the counsel will help the counselee to clarify life and handle the confusion that many experiences bring. When the counsel is instructive, inspirational, and supportive, it helps to "center" people for decisions and actions that count. In light of the pastor's need to serve these ends, and serve them well, sound training for this work is a must. Most seminaries rightly require preachers to prepare themselves for this through courses in pastoral care and counseling, as well as clinical pastoral education work.

As a third strategy for teaching from a pastoral perspective, the practical value of *teaching a class in the church program* should not be overlooked. Given the teaching responsibility that devolves upon the ordained minister who pastors a people, and given the investment of years in study for the ministerial role, it is not too much to expect the pastor to view the congregation as a school in Christian living and labor. Some pastors regularly teach a "Pastor's Class" of new Christians, new members, or young people. Some engage the entire congregation in guided study under their tutelage, either to examine a biblical theme or book or to examine some issue from a biblical perspective. But whether done with the whole congregation or within a small group session, the face-to-face approach permits a sense of partnership in learning and a sense of togetherness in being under the authority of the Word of God.

The fundamental work of the Christian pastor and a congregation of believers is to interpret the significance of the Christian faith for all of life, and to develop a Christian consciousness out of which agape love, the concerns of justice, and the Christian witness can be effectively applied in the world. The concerned pastor will be alert to the need for resources, methods, and occasions for fostering an ordered approach to this perennial task, always eager to effect greater competency in this necessary work of the church.

Ultimately, however, *the pastor will teach most influentially through personal Christian character and earnest example.* The accent here is on a personal life that can instruct by its integrity and disciplined direction.

Early in the twentieth century, R. P. Wyche called attention to the need for this, writing about the imperative for social uplift and advancement among the people: "The character and the ability of the [person] in the pulpit will determine its nature and extent."[14] This comment was but one from many concerned clergy reminding each other about this moral and spiritual demand for ministry. Now, at the latter end of the century, the same emphasis is being restated because the need for integrity and guardedness remains the same.

Harold A. Carter, a well-known African American preacher and scholar who prepared for ministry at several of the nation's leading theological seminaries, wrote, "I never heard the instructor in Christian ethics lecture on the basic morality that ought to be part and parcel of the Christian ministry."[15] Aware that the need for moral character was too important and necessary to be overlooked or left unmentioned, Carter devoted a chapter to the subject in his book *Myths That Mire the Ministry.* Warning against concupiscence, which he defines as "that desire for temporal ends which has its seat in the senses" and by which "the higher faculties of human life are subordinated to the lustful desires of the flesh," Carter further stated, "Since sex presents such a formidable problem in ministerial ranks, an in-depth study of its impact on this calling would be a blessing in seminary circles."[16] Many seminaries have begun including such a study among their required courses.

Some of those studies include an inquiry into the problems of sexual promiscuity as not only a failure in morals but also sometimes a behavior disorder or addiction. Seminarians taking such courses are guided in studying themselves existentially, with a focus on understanding entanglements, the influence of moods, temptation, the problem of viewing other persons as objects, and the problem of low self-esteem that manifests itself in seeking to control others. The root causes behind moral failure are also isolated, and the importance of learning to live morally and responsibly with others is underscored. Given the scope and import of ministry, a serious look at one's self and the potential problem areas about which ordained ministers, as both persons and professionals, must be aware has been increasingly necessary. The ultimate response a vital ministry demands of us is that of a God-committed selfhood coupled with spiritual empowerment. One is not likely to rightly deliver the word of truth to others, regarding sexual morality, until one has reached a mature understanding of one's own failings and feelings in this area. Given the primary emphasis upon sex in our society, this is not an area of teaching that preachers can disregard. Nor can they live as if they are helpless against the mores of society when these mores collide with the Word and the will of God.

In isolating some of the elements that make up a solid moral life for the ordained minister, John Malcus Ellison wrote, "Sincerity, honesty, unselfishness, loyalty to principle, truth, and integrity have no substitutes in the religious leader. . . . The Lord requires clean hands and honest hearts for his work."[17]

III

It has become rather commonplace to hear some pastor endorsed as a "great leader," meaning that he or she mixes well with people and handles leadership responsibilities with timeliness and adequacy. Many preachers view that "great leader" image as worthy of their concern and effort, as something to be attained as the capstone of their professional quest. But the serious pastor will be mindful of the need to *develop* leaders and not be content with only being viewed as one. This requires the work of teaching others.

Jesus of Nazareth showed the way in this as in all other necessary areas. Concerned about the future of the work to which he set himself, Jesus envisioned, selected, and trained a small group to expand and perpetuate his ministry as teacher, preacher, and healer. The demands upon him had become excessive and unending, and he had not come to stay. Aware that he had an impact on a growing number of followers, Jesus finally identified and isolated from within the crowds those who seemed reasonably gifted for what he would require of them. According to Luke 6:12-13, when that time came for Jesus to single out those persons from the crowd and shape them for assignments under his direction, Jesus withdrew to pray about the choices he had to make. He prayed about it throughout the night. The account tells us that when day came, he called his disciples and chose twelve of them. The Gospels tell us about subsequent training of the twelve, and underscore the time and guidance Jesus gave in shaping them for leadership. Jesus was sensible about the work assigned to his hands, and he chose and developed others to assist him in handling tasks that are still required in each generation. The wise pastor will think not only about the present but also about the future, and will teach others with that future in view.

I am reminded of a wise word I heard as a student at Oberlin Graduate School of Theology many years ago. Roger Hazelton, our seminary dean, told us that the truly effective pastor is not only someone who can take oversight in a church but also someone who can share insight with that church. He added, "Mark this: people in our churches today need more than strength for the mastery of life; they need light on the mystery of life; and there is a positive relationship between the two. In the last analysis you cannot have the one without the other."[19]

The interest to become a "great leader" will certainly continue within the various church traditions and will, in some persons, obscure a clear view of the solid work required of the serious Christian pastor. But those who concern themselves as true traditioners and helpers of the people will seek to show by example and teaching the meaning and power of the Christian faith. The issues people face demand from us informational and inspirational preaching, sound biblical counsel, times of strategic learning, and an honest modeling of what the Christian faith makes possible in human experience. Those who love the Lord and are deeply concerned to help people learn to live by the will of God will be intent, like the clerk from Oxford in Chaucer's *Canterbury Tales*, to "gladly teach" while following that teaching themselves.

NOTES

1. Among the many instances, see Matthew 26:25, 49; Mark 9:5; 11:21; 14:45. In John 1:38 we see the writer's concern to interpret the Aramaic by using the Greek *didaskalos* for "Teacher."
2. See Romans 6:17-19; Philippians 4:8-9; Titus 2:1-8, and 2 Peter 1:2-8, in particular.
3. Charles H. Dodd insisted that the New Testament writers drew a clear distinction between preaching and teaching, and that this was characteristic of early Christian usage. See his *Apostolic Preaching and Its Developments* (New York: Harper and Bros., 1960), p. 7. But for a

scholar who argued the case that a more balanced correspondence between these terms can be traced, see Robert H. Mounce, *The Essential Nature of New Testament Preaching* (Grand Rapids, Mich.: William B. Eerdmans, 1960), p. 42. See also Robert C. Worley, *Preaching and Teaching in the Earliest Church* (Philadelphia: Westminster Press, 1967), pp. 3-86.

4. See J. N. D. Kelly, *A Commentary on the Pastoral Epistles: 1 Timothy, 2 Timothy, Titus* (New York: Harper and Row, 1963) p. 766; see also p. 190 on 2 Timothy 2:24.

5. See Gerald E. Knoff, "The Churches Expect a Teaching Ministry," in *The Minister and Christian Nurture*, ed. Nathaniel F. Forsyth (Nashville: Abingdon Press, 1957), pp. 9-26; Floyd V. Filson, "The Christian Teacher in the First Century," *Journal of Biblical Literature* 60 (1941): pp. 317-28; James D. Smart, *The Teaching Ministry of the Church* (Philadelphia: Westminster Press, 1954), ch. 1, especially pp. 13-19; Robert C. Worley, *Preaching and Teaching in the Earliest Church*, especially pp. 131-51; Clark M. Williamson and Ronald J. Allen, *The Teaching Minister* (Louisville, Ky.: Westminster/John Knox Press, 1991), especially pp. 47-64.

6. Henry Sloan Coffin, *What to Preach: The Warrack Lectures for 1926* (New York: George H. Doran, 1926), pp. 12-13.

7. From among many examples that illustrate this, see especially Dewitte Holland, Jess Yoder, and Hubert Vance Taylor, eds., *Preaching in American History: Selected Issues in the American Pulpit, 1630–1967* (Nashville: Abingdon Press, 1969), and the companion volume, Holland, Yoder, and Taylor, eds., *Sermons in American History: Selected Issues in the American Pulpit, 1630–1967* (Nashville: Abingdon Press, 1971); Alfred T. Davies, ed., *The Pulpit Speaks on Race* (Nashville: Abingdon Press, 1965); R. Frederick West, *Preaching on Race* (St. Louis: The Bethany Press, 1962).

8. Albert C. Outler, "The Sense of Tradition in the Ante-Nicene Church," in *The Heritage of Christian Thought: Essays in Honor of Robert Lowry Calhoun*, eds. Robert E. Cushman and Egil Grislis (New York: Harper & Row, 1965), p. 9.

9. On the theme of social accommodation as it related to African American churches during an earlier period in American history, see Benjamin E. Mays, *The Negro's God: As Reflected in His Literature* (New York: Atheneum Edition, 1968), esp. pp. 14-16, 19-96.

10. Cited by Arthur J. Gossip, "The Whole Counsel of God: The Place of Biblical Doctrine in Preaching," *Interpretation* 1, no. 3 (July 1947), pp. 329-30.

11. Howard Thurman, *Jesus and the Disinherited* (Nashville: Abingdon-Cokesbury Press, 1919), p. 50.

12. Ibid, pp. 30-31.

13. See Wayne E. Oates, *The Christian Pastor* (Philadelphia: Westminster Press, 1982, third edition), in whose work is found a fundamental description of the Christian pastor's task and meaning from the perspective of the biblical doctrine of humanity and the Christian revelation of the nature of God. On the concept of levels of pastoral care, see especially chs. 6 and 7. See also a helpful critique of Oates's concept and methods by Walter C. L. Jackson II, "The Oates Agenda for Pastoral Care," in *Spiritual Dimensions of Pastoral Care*, eds. Gerald L. Borchert and Andrew D. Lester (Philadelphia: Westminster Press, 1985), pp. 119-41. For an additional and earlier critique of Oates' theological approach to pastoral counseling, see James N. Lapsley, in "Pastoral Theology Past and Present," in *The New Shape of Pastoral Theology: Essays in Honor of Seward Hiltner*, ed. William B. Oglesby Jr. (Nashville: Abingdon Press, 1969), esp. pp. 38-39, 44.

14. R. P. Wyche, "To What Extent Is the Negro Pulpit Uplifting the Race?" in *Twentieth Century Negro Literature*, ed. Daniel W. Culp (Atlanta: J. L. Nichols & Co., 1902), p. 122.

15. Harold A. Carter, *Myths That Mire the Ministry* (Valley Forge: Judson Press, 1980), p. 11.

16. Ibid., p. 44.

17. John Malcus Ellison, *They Who Preach* (Nashville: Broadman Press, 1965), pp. 5, 7.

18. Roger Hazelton, "And Gladly Teach—The Ministry Reconsidered," *Chicago Theological Seminary Register* 50, no. 8 (November 1960), p. 3.

PART THREE

INTO ALL
THE WORLD

CHAPTER NINE

J. Alfred Smith Sr.

PREACHING IN

URBAN AMERICA

Living just enuf, just enuf, for the City; livin'.
—*Stevie Wonder, "Living for the City"*

Preaching in urban America is exciting. It is exciting because it is challenging. The challenge is caused by the ever-changing faces and clashing cultural points of view that comprise the preaching audience. In one congregation, the Allen Temple Baptist Church of Oakland, California, where I preach weekly to an average of two thousand persons, there are Asians, Africans, African Americans, Anglos, Haitians, and Latinos. Some are the working poor; others are middle-class and are owners of businesses or respected achievers in their professions. Each worship service has its unique challenge.

People who come to each of the services bring their own unique needs, hopes, fears, backgrounds, languages, and cultural worldviews. Given this diversity and the widely known concerns that define the urban landscape, how does one preach in urban America today? What type of preaching is up to the task? For an answer we turn to a discussion of three of the inseparable ingredients of the preaching moment: context, content, and form.

Context

Urbanites live in cities where meanness is more dominant than mercy and where politicians punish victims for their plight. Persons are fighting for survival in situations where the strong preserve their advantages at the expense of the poor who exist hand-to-mouth in an impersonal mass of namelessness and facelessness. There appear to be no ground rules or societal boundaries or stability. The media blitzes urbanites daily with the worst of the world. We live in what scholars call the era of postmodernism. Craig Skinner, in his essay, "Between the Hippopotamus and the Crocodile: Locating an Age-Relevant Pulpit Within A Post-Modern World," says: "Our century has not been one noted for the hoped-for peace and justice which liberalized and secular thinkers believed such a publication would nourish. Our times place us in a world mainly materialistic and secular. International tensions have nurtured a rash of wars and current injustice, oppression, and genocide range from Bosnia to Haiti. The disillusionment and negative philosophy of post-modernism have influenced many urban dwellers to turn toward drugs, alcohol, and worse to deaden their feelings of nihilism and existential dread."[2] Still others have turned to a new age philosophy of pop psychology and talk show wisdom, cults, feel-good religions, or modified versions of Eastern religions, especially Buddhism.

Black preaching and all effective preaching is contextual, and it brings together in a moving synthesis the immanent and the transcendent. It is both this-worldly and otherworldly. It talks about life after death and life after birth. It addresses "the nasty now and now" and "the sweet bye and bye" in a dynamic tension that gives people the strength to celebrate while suffering. Urbanites will not return Sunday after Sunday to hear boring, abstract preachers speak as if God is in heaven and all is right with the world. So it is critical that one understands the context in which he or she preaches.

The suburban voice posits the overarching question, "I wonder what the future holds?" The urban voice posits the overarching question, "Will I make it to tomorrow?" Both locations do what all locations do: they enforce and reinforce the general mind-set and voice of the location. Therefore people in locations that portend a bright future expect or look forward to such a future. They expect a savings portfolio, houses, pensions, and long-term planning. Those in the other location do not expect a bright future or perhaps expect no future at all, as they are consumed by just getting through the moment. They expect no savings accounts (or a very small savings account), no apartments (except maybe subsidized housing), no pension (if a job at all), no long-term dreaming (except maybe of places such as heaven).

An understanding of the impact of context on the psyche of parishioners helps preachers to know how to address audiences where they are. Current context and a history of oppression, among other reasons, explain why Black religious expressions seem to have greater affinities with the Exodus story than with the Bethlehem story. They have more affinity with the delivery of Daniel from the den of lions and the saving of "the Hebrew boys" from the fiery furnace than they have with Peter, James, and John.[3]

Content

Given the context, what can be postulated about the content of urban American preaching? There are at least two things. First, the communication of content is occurring in an unambiguous, concrete atmosphere. Second, the content comes forth in an atmosphere of continuous suffering. Since this is the unmistakable urban environment, what is the urban gospel? Does it differ from a gospel of the suburbs, where there are well-manicured lawns and where graffiti rarely offends the eye?

Surely the content of the suburban gospel will not suggest that suffering is nonexistent in the surburban context, nor that its context totally lacks concreteness. What is the difference? More than thirty years of preaching have made me certain of at least two things: the *urban and suburban gospel are exactly the same* (in that they consist of a message that is healing, empowering, instructional, and theologically sound), *yet they are totally different* (because they occur in very different contexts)! The difference is one of degrees.

Effective urban preaching has a holistic presentation of Jesus as the core of its content. This Jesus is not the gospel preached by those who preach a gospel of prosperity or a nationalistic gospel of a Christ created by culture. It is the good news of Jesus the liberator, who said,

The Spirit of the Lord is upon me,
    because he has chosen me to bring good news to the poor.
He has sent me to proclaim liberty to the captives
    and recovery of sight to the blind,
to set free the oppressed
    and announce that the time has come
    when the Lord will save his people.

(Luke 4:18 GNB)

Effective urban preaching takes Professor James Cone seriously when he says that the content of contemporary preaching must start with the Incarnation of Jesus Christ. We also have to preach Jesus as our atonement at the cross of Calvary. We cannot ignore all of the political and sociological issues, in addition to the ecclesiastical issues, that brought about Jesus' death just outside the city limits of Jerusalem. Liberal scholars escape the ethical, existential, and eschatological dimensions of Jesus' life and death, as well as our own search for sanity in a sea of postmodern morality and ideological reality, by heavily emphasizing the concept of "The Christ of Faith" or the postresurrection narratives of Jesus apart from the doctrine of the Incarnation. But, as Cone argues, so must we preach that

> the transcendent can be encountered only in the particularity of a human situation. What ever else the transcendent may mean, it is always relevant to and for human beings. This is the significance of the Incarnation, God becoming human in Jesus. To be sure the sociological without the theological reduces the church to a social club of like minded people. But the theological without a critical sociological component makes the church a non-historical, spiritual community whose existence has no effect on our social and political environment.[4]

Form

Preaching audiences in urban America are dynamic and varied, and they challenge their preachers to become serious students of the art of communication. They are clamoring for a word that will help them make some sense of it all, or at least provide them with methods to cope. Accordingly, sermons cannot afford to be lectures or monologues. Sermons must be living, moving conversations that involve both the preacher and the audience in interchange, exchange, acceptance, rejection, and transformation. It takes the dynamics of the Holy Spirit, the preacher, and the audience to make sermons acceptable in today's urban world. Additionally, audiences are most helped by the use of everyday concrete language. Professor Henry Mitchell writes,

> Most credentialed pastors arrive at their first parishes having been for three or four years acculturated away from the vocabulary and mental images, the frame of reference and basic concerns of that portion of the population which seminaries and others have pilloried as the "silent majority."[5]

Dr. Mitchell is correctly suggesting that in order to communicate effectively, preachers who are trained to think logically and speak abstractly must move into the everyday world of the culture in which their congregations live.

Dr. Mitchell has also said that nothing important should ever be said by syllogism which is not also stated more comprehensively in symbolic story, poetry, or picture. Stories, analogies, and images formed the core and substance of the preaching of Jesus. The gospel writers present Jesus to us as a masterful storyteller. Stories are easy to remember. They involve us emotionally in the plot; they stimulate us to identify with the characters; and they can transform our thinking and change our character. An image is a word picture of a story or analogy. The preached image sticks in our minds and touches our hearts. The late Christian Methodist Episcopal Bishop Joseph Johnson, when describing the skills of the premier Black urban preachers he had heard, said,

> Black preaching is by its nature a storytelling process. And Black preachers have mastered the art of breathing life into both the story and the truth it teaches. He/she uses his/her imagination creatively and he/she places himself/herself as an eye witness to the story which he/she narrates and has mastered the art of role playing.[6]

In his seminal work, *Black Preaching*, Henry Mitchell gives examples of role playing by classic masters such as the late Dr. Sandy Ray. In illustrating how these masters used role playing in making Jesus Christ the substance and content of their communication, Dr. Mitchell shared two important hermeneutical principles: "[O]ne must declare the gospel in the language and culture of the people . . . [and] the gospel must speak to the contemporary man and his needs."[7] Stories, analogies, and images are stylistic forms for effective cross-cultural preaching in the urban world of today; more will be said later about cross-cultural preaching and ministry.

In an era of postmodern ambiguity, new metaphors, similes, and images are needed to effectively communicate the story of Jesus. Metaphors, similes, and images that have been a vital part of my own preaching tradition and spiritual faith journey—Jesus as the rose of Sharon, a battle-ax in a time of war, or a high tower, for instance—are barely recognizable to many of today's younger worshipers. Accordingly, while such images may enhance the comfort level of the speaker and those who are similarly situated, they do little, if anything, to reach many listeners.

Jesus as liberator is a reconstituted metaphor and image that is particularly meaningful to today's urbanites. This Jesus who liberates is the one who is among us in our everyday situation. Jesus as liberator is attractive because he offers urbanites life after birth. In a postmodern world of cynicism and disillusionment, people cannot identify with a high Christology that places their savior too far above or distant from their reach or portrays him as an abstraction. Jesus as liberator comes to persons at their point of need; even if they live in an environment where others fear to tread. He gives sense and soul to living and these urbanites can hardly wait for next Sunday to arrive so that they can hear such good news proclaimed again.

In his important book *The Search for Christian Credibility*, Alvin C. Porteous offers those who preach in our urban world some postmodern images of Christ. One metaphor that merits discussion is Porteous's reconstitution of the "neighbor" metaphor. He calls Jesus "The Gracious Neighbor." He reminds us that "Christ comes into our cities of alienation and fear today, as he did in the days of his flesh, as none other than the gracious neighbor. He stands alongside all the 'wretched of the earth' as their servant and as their fellow-sufferer."[8]

In urban America, use of the liberated, gracious neighbor as a paradigm is particularly effective. The acceptance of such a paradigm, however, will only become real in the lives of parishioners if it is preached and *lived* out. New metaphors, similes, and images not only must be used during the preaching moment, but it is also mandatory that we move with them beyond the pulpit and into the city that needs unconditional love. What are examples of a liberated, gracious neighbor in action? On Easter Sunday, 1994, Jews, Black Muslims, and Christians shared the Allen Temple Pulpit. The spirit was present working for reconciliation in an unreconciled world. In 1992, Huey Newton, the founder of the Black Panthers, was eulogized from the Allen Temple Pulpit, as have been police officers slain in the line of duty and drug pushers killed in urban drug wars. The liberated, gracious neighbor has built housing for seniors, for the homeless, and for those with AIDS. Preaching must happen in accord with the ministry of mercy and grace to those who are rejected by society but accepted by Jesus.

Preaching in urban America is challenging; thus it is paramount that each proclaimer understands the role of the inseparable three elements—context, content, and form. Yes, the task is challenging, but the God who calls preachers to this ministry also equips them.

Conclusion

Coming closer to Jesus Christ and endeavoring to preach Jesus as liberator and gracious neighbor in East Oakland, California, has called for more than a superficial understanding of cross-cultural ministry as a recent, popular theological term. It has meant welcoming Latino newcomers into the community and the church. The Reverend Rueben Hurtado, a pastor from Mexico, became the Latino Pastor at Allen Temple, and preaches every Sunday at one of three worship services. He is an integral member of the pastoral team. The Reverend Betita Coty has joined our pastoral team as the Latino Outreach Pastor. Both Pastor Hurtado and Pastor Coty have helped me develop skills in cross-cultural communication.

Those who are committed to preaching in the urban centers of America in the twenty-first century are persons who will study cross-cultural and multicultural communication. In December 1994, the

Allen Temple Baptist Church held an ll:l5 A.M. worship service in honor of Latino leaders in Oakland. While I preached in Spanish, Reverend Betita Coty gave the English translation. As an example of preaching in urban America today, the English translation of the sermon and prayer is reprinted here.

GOD AND THE NIGHT SHIFT

And there were shepherds living out in the fields nearby, keeping watch over their flocks at night."
—Luke 2:8 NIV

These were the best of times and the worst of times. Beggars and royalty, the powerful and the powerless, the educated and the ignorant, the godly and ungodly were all under the rule of the Roman government. Doors were locked and fireplaces extinguished. It was the hour of the night shift, and creatures stirred, but barely. The stars in their sockets lit up the black sky like diamonds. The moon, adorned in a silver robe, presided over the night. A silent breeze dropped by for the evening. While the masses slept, some were working the night shift.

I. Shepherds Were Working the Night Shift

Saint Luke tells us there were shepherds out in the fields nearby, keeping watch over their flocks this night. Poor shepherds—chilled and alone, low wages and long hours. Poor shepherds—no health care, and no hope, no respect or justice, on the night shift.

Shepherds of today, though called by different names, live like shepherds of yesterday. They work the night shift. They are the last hired and the first fired. They are demeaned because of their color and their culture, their language and their living conditions. These shepherds do the dirty work that others refuse to do. They have not claimed any clout and they have no disposable income. They plant corn and pick grapes. They change the beds where others sleep, and as nannies, it's others' children they keep. They work the night shift, *but they are not alone.*

II. God Works the Night Shift

Angelic ambassadors bring to Saint Luke's shepherds good news. The good news is that the God who neither sleeps nor slumbers has a preference for the poor. They are high on the Almighty's agenda. God loves all, but stands with and stands up for the poor and the oppressed. And God works the night shift.

God has long worked the night shift. Ever since God breathed life into humanity, God has always peered down from the high tower of heaven to keep watch. One night God saw a Pharaoh plotting conquest at the Red Sea, and God made an appointment for the wind. One night, God saw human bones in a valley and selected a prophet to make them live again. One night, God saw a teenager and made her an unwed mother and blessed among women.

III. The Good News of the Night Shift

The Christmas message is the ultimate good news from the night shift. The God of the night shift sent a baby to a manger in Bethlehem. This son lived on meager fare, was shunned by the status quo and betrayed by bosom friends. This son, who was so denied, became the chief cornerstone. And on him all can now hang their cares, because he cares for all, especially those who are on the night shift.

And because of this son, we are one. Jesus the liberator, Jesus our lifeline, Jesus the lily of the valleys, makes us one. Color, countries, education, earnings, and power divide us. But Jesus makes us one. Because of this baby from Bethlehem, Red, Brown, Black, Yellow, and White can all be one. We are the recipients of this good news, this amazing grace. Gladly we can tell it on the mountain, in the Oakland Hills, the housing projects, and everywhere. Joy to the world, the savior, who came to break down barriers and make us one, has come. Peace on earth and to all goodwill.

NOTES

1. Craig Skinner, "Between the Hippopotamus and the Crocodile: Locating an Age-Relevant Pulpit Within A Post-Modern World," in *Between The Hippopotamus and The Crocodile* (Durham, N.C.: The Academy of Homiletics, 1994), pp. 1-2.
2. Henry Mitchell, *The Recovery of Preaching* (San Francisco: Harper & Row, 1977), pp. 45-47.
3. James H. Cone, *Speaking the Truth: Ecumenism, Liberation and Black Theology* (Grand Rapids, Mich.: William B. Eerdmans, 1986), p. 115.
4. Mitchell, *The Recovery of Preaching*, p. 145.
5. Joseph Johnson Jr., *Proclamation Theology* (Shreveport, La.: Fourth Episcopal District Press, 1977), p. 48.
6. Henry H. Mitchell, *Black Preaching* (Philadelphia and New York: J. B. Lippincott, 1970), p. 29.
7. Alvin C. Porteous, *The Search for Christian Credibility* (Nashville: Abingdon Press, 1971), pp. 118-19.

Richard F. Ward

B E Y O N D

T E L E V A N G E L I S M

PREACHING ON THE
PATHWAY TO RITUAL
RE-FORMATION

Rites deteriorate. Entropy is the rule; therefore, they must be raised up constantly from the grave of book, body, memory, and culture.
> —*Ronald L. Grimes*, Beginnings in Ritual Studies

Television preachers are not as successful as they are because people crave obscurantist ideas; people just want some warmth and spontaneity, something that speaks to the entire being.
> —*Henry H. Mitchell*, Black Preaching: The
> Recovery of a Powerful Art

*There resides, in the consciousness of virtually every-*one who preaches these days, an image of an "electronic preacher." He (or she, though it is rare) mediates popular criteria for good public speaking in our culture: an attractive, expressive face, a voice that can modulate from an indignant shout to quiet assurance, a charismatic (and well-crafted) persona that courts, cajoles, and compels. The electronic preacher's presence is part of the environment of symbols that surround us and is a reminder of the iconic power of electronic technology in our culture. Our responses to this phantom may vary: some of us may long for this unwelcome image to be finally exorcised and forgotten, others have cultivated indifference or perhaps serious dialogue with it, still others compete with or even imitate it as a model of effective communication. Whatever our responses to the morals or methods of the electronic preacher, his pervasive and symbolic presence shapes, whether positively or negatively, our culture's perception of religious communication.

Theological education has largely ignored the electronic preacher because it has not known how to establish the study of communications in the theological curriculum. A "transportation" or "transmissions" metaphor still dominates the theological school's approach to communications and thus to preaching. "They see communication as a process of transmitting messages at a distance for the purpose of control. Communication is persuasion, attitude change, behavior modification, socialization through the transmission of information, influence, or conditioning."[1] While this model dominates, the communicative work of the preacher will continue to be construed as the preparation of a "package,"[2] containing a message, which is then delivered through acquired vocal and physical behaviors to a group of passive listeners.

The "transmissions" metaphor was useful in typographic culture because it offered some techniques for helping preachers lift words from a page and release them into acoustical space.[3] While stressing the importance of animation in the art of preaching, it nevertheless blinded us to the way communication actually works in culture and made intrinsic connections between theology and communications very difficult to make. Consequently, those who preach to an increasingly electronic culture are not as certain how to "read" television as they are a biblical text. They are left bewildered, as the undercurrents unleashed by telecommunications erode the ground where they stand to preach. They are losing control.

Educational practice based upon this model is reduced to skill and technique building, and is quickly relegated to the margins of a theological curriculum.[4] Let us finally declare the bankruptcy of the "transmissions" or "transportation" metaphor in the study of communications so that we can better understand what it means to preach while the television, talk radio, Oprah, grunge rock, and even Christian music are all "turned on." In contrast, James Carey in his "ritual" view, has offered a more potent metaphor for studying communications in an electronic culture:

> communication is viewed as a process through which a shared culture is created, modified, and transformed. A ritual view of communication is not directed toward the extension of messages in space but the maintenance of society in time. [It is] not the act of imparting information or influence, but the creation, representation, and celebration of shared beliefs. If a transmission view of communication centers on the extension of messages across geography for purposes of control, a ritual view centers on the sacred ceremony that draws persons together in fellowship and commonality.[5]

Studying the relationship of communication to ritual gives us a better understanding of the media environment in which we live and minister and to which we proclaim and embody the gospel of Jesus Christ. It also locates the study of preaching where it belongs in the theological school: preaching must be understood as an "oral text" within Christian ritual and evaluated on the basis of its power (or lack thereof) to evoke the presence of the Holy Spirit.

Communication and Ritual Misapprehension

Unfortunately, the word *ritual* has poor connotations for many of us, especially when we are thinking about communicating a lively faith. Ritual seems to be the opposite of free and spontaneous celebration of the spirit and, on the surface, does not help us cultivate what Henry Mitchell has called a "language of possession."[6] The meteoric rise of the electronic preacher into our field of vision is symptomatic of a "ritual boredom" that pervades the structures of Protestant religious life.[7]

In response to an article he wrote on the electronic church for *TV Guide*,[8] William Fore received almost five hundred letters from readers testifying to why they participated in such a ministry. Reading and responding to these letters led Fore to write: "the perception of many mainline churches as dry, unfriendly, and moribund is not just a religious problem, for the vacuum that is created has spawned a crisis in the society as a whole."[9]

The 1980s and early 1990s were years of great experimentation with television as a means to address this boredom with the liturgical forms available in "established" churches. Preaching played a central role in this enterprise, though new modes of proclamation on the medium continue to diversify. Religious programs now feature "tearful soliloquies and 'heartfelt' renditions of gospel songs, testimonials, talk shows, variety programs and revivals," and thus are becoming less and less distinguishable from secular fare.[10]

What we have learned from these ongoing experiments in televangelism is that optimism about "packaging" the gospel and releasing it over the airwaves is not only naive, but is dangerous to the integrity of the gospel. Television is not "neutral." As Peter G. Horsfield points out in his book *Religious Television*, in order to sustain the necessary structures of financial support, the religious broadcaster has had to shape the presentations "according to the dictates of . . . business advisors rather than by the mandates of traditional theological sources."[11] The "oral gospels" according to television emphasize themes that fulfill the moods and desires of those who give financial support. God is magical and removed from the world, faith means having access to the miraculous power and financial resources for self-aggrandizement, and "practical" Christianity is effective only if it works toward self-fulfillment. Bill Fore charges that "this is true idolatry—to absorb the secular society's vision of success and self-centeredness and then justify it with a coating of verbal Christianity."[12] Discernment of mission in this wilderness of electronic gadgetry and marketing strategies has proved to be difficult indeed.

Televangelism endures not because it is effective evangelism or because it offers an alternative mythos to that of "secular" television. It endures because it has created yet another form of popular entertainment that is suited to and shaped by the demands of the medium; it is *the medium itself* that is fulfilling a religious role in culture.

The way through our predicament as a wilderness people means attending to the way television speaks to a ritually impoverished culture, and then to rediscover those places in the body of belief where Christian religion "excites the serious play of the soul and evokes the fullness of human passion."[13] Until we as Christian communities uncover some ritual pathways (such as those provided by some denominations of the Black church, for example) that will enable and empower us to do that, the television will continue to be on, giving culture its clues for how rituals should be performed.

Television as Ritual Communication

The function of ritual in any society is first to provide order to the mysterious chaos of experience, through image and displays of icons, through rhythmic sound, through movement and gesture, through narrative word and enactment of myth, and through reestablishment of oral, kinesthetic, and conceptual patterns by, in, and through a community. Second, ritual is the means by which individuals are either integrated, separated from, or reintegrated into "Other," experienced either as the whole community or as supernatural power. Its grammar, that is, the elements by which it accomplishes its communal, integrative work, includes willful participation by individuals through performance of formal speech and gesture, the creation (or re-creation) of specific spaces and the establishment of times, and certainly the enactment of some remembered event. If a culture is indeed ritually impoverished it is because "the rituals, in their form, content, and manner of performance, have lost touch with the actualities of people's lives and are thus simply arcane; or else the people have lost the ability to apprehend their very need of ritual, do not see what rituals are good for, and thus do not find them even potentially valuable."[14]

Television, and the expression of Christian religion that it privileges, has become a pervasive influence precisely because it has performed the function of ritual in our society. Through the use of skillfully produced images, sounds, and tight narrative lines, formulas, and dramatic situations, television grants easy access to a vast mythic world that has remarkable cogency. Fore maps this world around the following central values: the fittest survive, power moves from the center out, and both progress and material acquisition are inherently good.[15]

Advertisers have discovered how to use images and sounds to endow ordinary objects with powers of transformation and link them with perceived human needs. Purchasing a product opens the passageway to a fantasy world of unlimited abundance and prosperity. We orient ourselves to these values not by Kierkegaardian leaps into darkness but by playful engagement with the iconography of television, the most distinctive of which is the commercial. "Like traditional icons, commercials appeal to hope and fear. They even promise miracles. Their aim is to evoke in the viewer loyalty and conviction. Instead of fealty to king or savior, the fidelity is to products."[16] To belong to the happy company of the beautiful people who model for us everything from upbeat attitudes to styles of clothing is simply to purchase the product or at least to remember the jingle or slogan.

It is this kind of participation that grafts us into the "whole," the economic and political order and value structure of consumerism. And it is out from this context that the electronic preacher formulates and preaches the kind of "good news" that helps a listener feel included in the bright universe of television.

Implications: Preaching and Ritual Communication

In his play *The Chairs*, the late absurdist playwright Eugene Ionesco leaves us with a vivid image of our cultural landscape. The central characters are the Old Man and the Old Woman, who are awaiting the end of their lives in a large, sparsely furnished room. They spend their last hours playing make believe and telling stories, struggling to articulate "something to say . . . a message to communicate to humanity."[17] Feeling this to be a sacred duty, they have hired a professional Orator to come and speak to all humankind on their behalf. The action of the play accelerates with the impending arrival of the Orator. The Old Man and the Old Woman have invited everyone from janitors to bishops to post office employees, even the Pope and the Emperor will come to hear the Orator's great summation of the couple's life.

We hear sounds of the guests' arrival and watch the frantic pantomimic gestures of the exhausted couple as they perform their greetings. But the illusion of presence is poignantly conveyed: the space is filled with empty chairs. The Orator finally arrives. He is the only other "real" character in the play. The couple, fully entrusting their message to him, leap out of the window in a double suicide. The Orator steps up to the platform and stands before the audience of empty chairs. To our horror, we discover that he is mute. After vainly struggling to communicate, he writes some nonsense on the board, and exits.

Here is an image of the typographic church in television culture. Empty pantomimic gestures and archaic phrases describe the performance of ossified ritual that does not touch, in Henry Mitchell's phrase, the "depths of being, where faith and trust reside."[18] Like the Old Man and Old Woman in the company of phantoms, human beings wait in hope for an "experiential encounter,"[19] where the broken fragments and impressions of our intuitive and emotive and cognitive experiences are gathered up and connected to the "Other"—not just ourselves and our finitude.

Christians claim to have some good news about the tangible, enfleshed presence of this "Other." However, the church's way of speaking and enacting its gospel of Jesus Christ is often bound by the printed page. At a time when "Word" is shockingly present as color, sound, texture, spontaneity, story, and encounter, the typographic Christian church manages only to speak nonsense to an increasingly empty space. I am rooted in such a tradition and from this place have often felt the heartbreak of watching the typographic church stand in a space where "emptiness" is so profound and manages to utter only nonsensical distortions of its gospel.

The distance between the "new oralism"[20] arising with electronic culture and the persistent orality of Black rituals of worship is not so vast. Henry Mitchell notes that "the religious communication of Blacks has survived, for one reason, because it was not in the mainstream of the changing world of White theology and worship."[21]

It is still an open question whether the words, phrases, concepts, and images from Christian tradition can become television fare. Henry Mitchell and others have interpreted for the whole church a lively ritual and homiletical tradition that, since it has not been dependent upon print for its continuation, is a resource for worship practice in our postliterate, electronic era.

Electronic technology has eroded the print culture that shaped the primary communicative strategies of the liberal White church, Catholic and Protestant, contributing to a condition of ritual boredom and impoverishment. At the same time, television advertisers and broadcasters have assumed the quasi-religious role of providing rituals that orient us to the values of consumer culture. TV has even given birth to an electronic gospel that spiritualizes material acquisition and wealth and privileges sensational, privatized experiences of the supernatural. In the end, however, only a yawning spiritual emptiness remains. The mainline Catholic and Protestant churches, institutions historically and theologically oriented toward print culture, have been unable to speak the language of the "new oralism."

New rites, rituals, and ways of preaching, such as those developed by the Black church, must be resurrected out of the "new oralism" in culture and hermeneutical styles. Christian worship will become empowering instead of enervating only when spontaneous, unrehearsed interactions begin to open up new forms of personal participation. Perhaps the central figures in this renewal will not be preachers who design print-based, liturgical supports for sermons, but creative liturgists who preach. Liturgy in postliteracy will make Christ's presence manifest in the same manner that Jesus communicated the Word: through parable (often portrayed as drama), story and song, face-to-face interaction and dialogue, gesture, and sensory engagement.

Unlike the Orator in Ionesco's play, the postliterate liturgist-preacher will not be left to oratorical conventions that lie beyond his or her range of skills. One who is empowered by a Holy Spirit will not step into a landscape of phantom presences week after week. Once we are willing to look, we will discover sacred space in our homes, our places of worship, and our communities. Such spaces will be ritually marked as sacred because they will be filled with flesh-and-blood "actors," not illusions. The postliterate liturgist-preacher will be nourished by these who gather, both to enact and to partake of the Body, and who will recognize Christ's presence through storytelling, oral reading and singing, movement, and the display of image, symbol, icon, and vestment. Preaching to the whole person, recovering the orality of the Scripture, fashioning imaginative identifications with biblical characters, and fostering the creative partnership between preacher, listener, and Spirit, are riffs in the music of postliterate Christian worship.

Perhaps the electronic preacher has come into our consciousness, not to harangue us into stylistic or theological imitation, but to call us to ritual renewal. Perhaps we are *on the brink* of seeing a people of the page transformed into a people of the Word.

NOTES

1. James W. Carey, "Communication and Culture," *Communication Research* (April 1975): p. 177.
2. Walter Ong, "Communications Media and the State of Theology," *Cross Currents* 19 (1969): p. 463.
3. I use *typographic* as an adjective describing how spaces reserved for mass production of print shape the ways mainline Protestants think about "Word" and words. See Walter J. Ong, *Orality and Literacy: The Technologizing of the Word* (London and New York: Methuen, 1982), pp. 128-29, 135-38.
4. Peter S. Hawkins quotes a study by Jurgen Hilke on this very point. In a 1985 study of 198 theological schools in North America, Hilke observed that "communications" is almost exclusively interpreted as "skills acquisition and refinement" leading to the end product of making "better communicators" from the pulpit. He concludes that in the theological schools, "communication" as a field of study does not warrant serious attention (Peter S. Hawkins, "Communication at Yale Divinity School: A Feasibility Study," [Unpublished paper, 1990], 20-21.)
5. Carey, "Communication and Culture," p. 177.
6. Henry H. Mitchell, *Black Preaching: The Recovery of a Powerful Art* (Nashville, Abingdon Press, 1990), p. 124.
7. See Tom F. Driver, *The Magic of Ritual: Our Need for Liberating Rites that Transform Our Lives and Our Communities* (San Francisco: HarperSanFrancisco, 1991), pp. 7-8.
8. William F. Fore, "There Is No Such Thing as a TV Pastor," *TV Guide* (19-25 July 1980): pp. 15-18.
9. William F. Fore, *Television and Religion: The Shaping of Faith, Values, and Culture* (Minneapolis: Augsburg, 1987), pp. 99-100.
10. Quentin J. Schultz, "Balance or Bias? Must TV Distort the Gospel?" *Christianity Today* (18 March 1988): p. 29.
11. Peter G. Horsfield, *Religious Television: The American Experience* (New York: Longman, 1984), pp. 34-35.
12. Fore, *Television and Religion*, p. 113.
13. Gregor T. Goethals, *The TV Ritual: Worship at the Video Altar* (Boston: Beacon Press, 1981), p. 144.
14. Driver, *The Magic of Ritual*, p. 7.
15. Fore, *Television and Religion*, pp. 65-66.
16. Goethals, *The TV Ritual*, p. 137.
17. Eugene Ionesco, *Four Plays*, trans. Donald M. Allen (New York: Grove Press, 1958), p. 119.
18. Henry H. Mitchell, *Celebration and Experience in Preaching* (Nashville: Abingdon Press, 1990), p. 19.
19. Ibid., p. 25.
20. Walter Ong defines this "new oralism" as a quality of human communication that is not dependent upon print but arises out of the communicative values of electronic media, including spontaniety, unrehearsed reactions, conversational casualness, and an existential focus on the present. See his "Communications Media and the State of Theology," *Cross Currents* 19 (1969): pp. 462-80.
21. Mitchell, *Black Preaching: The Recovery of a Powerful Art*, p. 19.

Works Consulted but Not Cited

Brilioth, Yngve. *A Brief History of Preaching*. Translated by Karl E. Mattson. Philadelphia: Fortress Press, 1965.
Rice, Charles L. *The Embodied Word: Preaching as Art and Liturgy*. Minneapolis: Fortress Press, 1991.

CHAPTER ELEVEN

Barbara Harris

CAN THE CITY BE SAVED?

(OR WHY IS THERE A
CHURCH ON EVERY
CITY CORNER?)

> *Seek the welfare of the city where I have sent you into exile, and*
> *pray to the LORD on its behalf, for in its welfare you will find your*
> *welfare.*
> —*Jeremiah 29:7 (NRSV)*

*T*he prophet Jeremiah's revolutionary counsel to the exiles in Babylon holds meaning for the church and the people who inhabit today's cities. For indeed churches—through their clergy and laity—have a crucial role to play in addressing the myriad problems contributing not only to the physical but also to the spiritual and moral decay of our cities.

Stumbling Block and Opportunity

The two questions raised by the title of this essay present both a stumbling block and an opportunity. Possible answers to both questions—Can the city be saved? and Why is there a church on every city corner?—take us to the heart of the social gospel to which Henry Mitchell and many of his colleagues have been so diligently committed throughout their years of urban ministry.

There are many forces in church and society that are diverting clergy from a clear vision of what we are called to be and do as urban ministers in this time of trial, tribulation, chaos, and change. Some of these forces are seductive, process-oriented redefinitions of our context, the apparent logic of which could lead us into endless debates about how to do what we should do, rather than enabling us to do it.

The present context has been well-described by Loren B. Mead in his 1992 book, *The Once and Future Church*. Mead's work draws our attention, in the author's own words, to "how our vision of the mission of the church came into sharp focus . . . what that vision produced . . . how that clarity came to lose its sharp focus . . . an emerging sense of mission and . . . the kinds of changes that will require [re]ordering our lives within the church."[1]

Our context, according to Mead, is marked by the rapidly fading "Christendom Paradigm" that began to emerge in the fourth century, beginning with the conversion of Emperor Constantine in A.D. 313 and which until recently has held appreciable sway in the church. "Unlike earlier Christian communities, the church, after Constantine, identified with the Empire. There was no separation between the world and the church, between the sacred and secular. Imperialism and mission were inseparable."[2]

The importance for us of that shifting paradigm, Mead observes, "lies in the fact that most of the generation that now leads our churches grew up with it"—perhaps not so much in its ancient and classical versions, but in its nineteenth- and early twentieth-century manifestations—"as a way of thinking about church and society. And all the structures and institutions that make up the churches and the infrastructure of religious life . . . are built on its presuppositions."[3]

The Dulling of an Edge

But the church, particularly as represented by the Catholic and mainline Protestant denominations, appears to have lost its edge because it has lost its way. As *Newsweek* reported a few years ago, mainline Protestant churches are "gripped by a crisis: of identity and loyalty, membership and money, leadership and organization, culture and belief. . . . For more than a century, [mainline Protestant] denominations helped define America and its values. Now they are struggling to define themselves" as they "are running out of money, members and meaning."[4]

One of the primary reasons for this loss of edge and loss of way in the church has to do with the *cultural captivity of the gospel.* In this process individuals and groups seek to use the church to legitimate their own identity, power, and status rather than seeking to transform their identity, power, and status to the demands of the gospel. Seen in this light, the continued racial segregation in the church in this country is one clear and vivid example of this cultural captivity. When understood for what it is, segregation is the root of much of the debate within churches over issues of inclusivity, traditional values, and fundamentalism. The latter are but surface issues that, at face value, constitute sources of discord, but in fact mask deeper cultural distinctions. The Black church runs the risk of succumbing to this Eurocentric cultural captivity that has made its peace with or has not sufficiently contended against racism, sexism, classism, and homophobia.

We in the church should stop fighting amongst ourselves over what should be the Christian worldview or, more precisely, over which is preeminent among the various worldviews that exist in Christianity. We would be better served to acknowledge that, like Paul, speaking on the plaza to the unknown God, we now confront a society that has little understanding or respect for any version of the Christian worldview! The failure to recognize this reality as our present context leads to deeper frustration and a sense of alienation for biblical fundamentalists—despite their growing numbers—and self-styled traditionalists in my own denomination. That frustration is a result of the world's rejection of their myopic and self-serving gospel. This is at the heart of the tension within churches between so-called traditionalists and those who are seeking to adapt the church and its message to the changing societal scene.

The answers to the questions posed by the title of this essay perhaps lie in our willingness to address the real questions of our disunity as faithful people. *Can Christians find anything at all to focus on as a uniting force?* Christ, we proclaim, is the answer to every question, but it is the diversity of the questions to which he is expected to be the answer that reveals our disunity, our fragmentation, and our inertia.

Re-Focus Focus Focus

Sadly, churches have been focused more on survival and charity than on justice, which is compassion or love distributed. Charity is the giving from one's surplus to the individual or cause of one's choice. It is usually painless and selective. But justice is sacrificial giving, or the process by which greater equity is established between individuals and groups. It rarely is painless, and in most instances it involves struggles for systemic change.

Some additional and easily recognizable distinctions are that charity usually is passive, supports the status quo, is low-risk, is superficial, can create enmity, is nonpolitical, pastoral, and individual. Justice, on the other hand, is active, brings about change, is nonselective, high-risk, systemic, long-term, political, prophetic, and collective.

The road from charity to justice, however, is marked by more questions than directional signs. If churches are to develop relevant ecclesial models for today, some of these questions must be addressed: Can one-dimensional social service ministries, which have been our history and mark much of our present practice, be maintained in the face of increasingly overwhelming need? At what point must charity cease and demands for systemic change commence? Can work for systemic change exist in isolation from the persons and situations for whom change is desired? What is the ecumenical option for such a time? While all of these questions are key to the restructuring of relevant and effective urban ministry, two in particular merit further comment.

Can systemic change exist in isolation from the persons and situations for whom change is desired? Whereas the two previous questions call us to a profound rearticulation of our spiritual values, which in turn will inform our economic, political, and social arrangements, this third question reminds us that these arrangements will have meaning only to the degree that they positively affect the lives of the hungry, the homeless, the sick and dying. Ivory-towered analysis without a firm grounding in the reality of human suffering is an affront to the people, and apocalyptic prognostications are more apt to engender a sense of powerlessness and paralysis than to inspire action that leads to redemption. What we need is not a politically correct but unworkable liberation theology. Rather, we need a liberation *methodology* that overcomes polarization, fosters true equality, and actually changes the lives and conditions of people.

What is the ecumenical option at this time? While all religious institutions are undergoing the same stress, is this not a time to come to some common understandings about priorities and responses? The old adage that two heads are better than one takes on new meaning in the crisis of change; we must stretch the limits of cooperation that new circumstances present. Whole sectors of human services are collapsing, including housing, education, health care, and welfare. Individual church bodies have at least three options. The first is to walk away from the situation and hope the storm will pass. The second is to expend all of their resources in one grand explosion of concern and then walk away. The third is to overcome issues of turf, polity, and ownership and become creative in reducing overhead so that maximum resources can be channeled into commonly agreed upon priorities over time. Although we may never live to see the full flowering of this vision, I lift it up as a reasonable option for all churches to consider.

Mainline denominations might be surprised to discover that they have much to learn from other churches about how to survive with meager resources, and non-mainline churches might have some creative suggestions about how to put the abundance of mainline churches to more practical use.

And a Child Shall Lead Us

One logical place to begin to address all of the foregoing questions is to look at the situation from the perspective of children and young people. Indeed, there are many who maintain that the most appropriate focus for urban ministry over the next eight to ten years is on children and youth. The social ills of the city impinge directly upon our children and young people in the most dramatic fashion. The world they will inherit will be shaped by how we address such issues now. Certainly one might look at the issues of economic justice, crime, and violence and at how they relate to the educational system, the criminal justice system, and the social welfare system. From there, one can quickly grasp how a youth- or child-focused ministry takes us to the heart of current social issues from a fresh perspective.

With the triumph of capitalism, market forces are most readily seen at work in the consumptive habits of young people, on the one hand, and the turf battles of street gangs, on the other. Understanding how young people's reality is, in fact, being determined by such forces, should challenge the church to begin to provide alternative visions and opportunities. Such initiatives must be coupled with work for genuine educational reform and social service delivery that is geared toward empowering persons and building rather than fracturing community.

William McKinney, writing in the *Christian Century* in 1989, noted, "Flawed and impossible though they may be at times, congregations are the most powerful antidote we have to the radical individualism that pervades American secular and religious culture."[5] In this regard the local congregation on every city corner can play an important role in building community. The congregation that cannot, should agree to *vacate the corner premises.*

Even if, in Kenneth Woodward's words, the church "runs out of money and members," it need not "run out of meaning"; and that meaning is not found in its bank account or the numbers on its membership rolls. The church's meaning may well be found in the development of a parallel spiritual vision and rule of life that lifts up the gospel imperative to work for a world in which (1) justice is the normative goal for the distribution of the world's resources; (2) equity is the normative goal of interpersonal and intra-group relations; (3) sustainability is the primary criteria for evaluating any economic or social system that would claim our participation and provide our means of survival; and (4) accessibility is the rule for participation in decision making. (We must constantly be asking the question, Who is not at the table but will be affected by the decision or the action that is proposed or is undertaken?)

With these four gospel imperatives as the foundation, the work that can be done for children is envisioned.

1. Justice is the normative goal for the distribution of the world's resources.

In order for the church to serve as a true advocate for children, it must revision the world. No longer can the world be viewed as the agenda establisher. The church need not set itself up *against* culture, but it can no longer continue to take its cues *from* culture. When the church talks of justice as a normative goal, it is not simply a matter of waving banners and preaching sermons against causes and entities that the *majority* agrees are wrong and detestable. The Bible and the works of Jesus are the point of departure for the church; inexorably tied to this book and this savior are people's lives, which can be changed because of both.

Because the church dares to be bound by objectives claiming justice for "the least of these," it must prepare for the inevitable confrontations from those who have much and are not willing to share without being forced. For them justice is admirable until it interferes with their agendas or their advantages. The church must dare to hold the greedy accountable. For such battles, we need more than theological treatises, spirited sermons, and marches of protest; we need conversion—conversion to or back to the teachings of the Bible and the ways of Jesus. Those who care about children can no longer acquiesce to those who find it acceptable that less than 10 percent of the people in America hold 90 percent of its wealth. To balance such an inequitable distribution of wealth will require demonstrations, education, and changes in legislation. But none of these will be seriously attended unless we are convinced (converted to the belief) that the Bible and the example set by Jesus demand a redistribution of resources.

2. Equity is the normative goal of interpersonal and intra-group relations.

If in the twenty-first century only one thing could be purged from the life of the church, it should be inequity in personal relationships. Within the church, especially where hierarchies exist, the educated dominate, the long-tenured dominate, and males dominate. Of course it could be called by many names (classism, capitalism, racism, sexism), but domination by any other name is still domination. If in Christ we are all one, then we are all equal. All have certain unalienable rights, and among these are *life* (not lives daily lived in the shadows of drive-by shootings and carjackings); *liberty* (not abnormal rates of incarceration, glass ceilings, and un-affirmative action; and *the pursuit of happiness* (not journeys stamped with hopelessness because they begin in poverty, illiteracy, and poor nurture).

Until we view each other as equal, equity will remain a phantom. We will continue to converse at work, but will still segregate our church services. We will buy the same products, but will not alter who does the majority of the advertising. We will agree to collectively mourn when federal buildings are bombed, but we will not hold serious debates on why we continue to disproportionately fill our prisons with persons who are non-White and uneducated.

3. Sustainability is the primary criteria for evaluating any economic or social system that would claim our participation and provide our means of survival.

Too often the church is guilty of holding on to programs that no longer work. We all know that churches could do a better job of fiscal management and church administration. But when I speak here of sustainability, I speak not simply of whether or not what we are doing is outdated or economically infeasible. Sustainability here concerns assessing whether or not the ministries in which we engage continuously exemplify the principles honored by Christ, to see if they are theologically correct and consider the revelations brought to us through the lives that our ministries seek to benefit.

Just as we cannot afford to sustain church programs and theologies that are wrong, outdated, and fiscally irresponsible, the church also needs to be concerned with its support of societal and economic systems that are outdated and unresponsive to "the least of these." We serve not only near stained glass windows, but also in the world. When Wall Street speaks of higher interest rates and the weakness of the dollar, when government speaks of revamping the welfare system, when technology speaks of the invasion of the information superhighway, where is the church? Are we there to voice our opinions as to whether or not these projects and developments can or should be sustained? If we are the advocates for and with those who are trying to gain their voices, then our voices must be heard in all sectors of society. The "Religious Right" has learned this point and spends its money and time accordingly.

4. Accessibility is the rule for participation in decision making.

I have chosen to focus on children as a rallying point for mission and urban ministry as we look toward the twenty-first century because we can all agree that children are important, but children provide the perfect focus for other reasons as well. As we glance at the great ecclesiastical circle, we notice the absence not only of children, but also of women, of the disabled, and of gays and lesbians. Just like children, women are not seen as meriting full partnership at the table. Just like children, the disabled are not considered desirable at the table. Just like children, gays and lesbians are not viewed as having the type of values that are desired at the table. But just as Jesus did, those of us in positions of power must dare to take sides with those who are "left out." For just as the Lord told Jeremiah that he would find his welfare by seeking the welfare of all within the city, so the Lord tells us.

The city would seem to have a church with a "soul-saving" agenda on almost every corner. But it is only when the church on every city corner sees itself as a *movement* committed to a Christ-centered agenda (justice, equity, sustainability, and accessibility), rather than as an *institution*, that the city and its inhabitants can be saved.

N O T E S

1. Loren B. Mead, *The Once and Future Church: Reinventing the Congregation for New Mission Frontiers* (Washington, D.C.: Alban Institute, 1992), p. 7.
2. Ibid., p. 13.
3. Ibid., p. 18.
4. Kenneth L. Woodward, "Dead End for the Mainline?" *Newsweek* (9 August 1993): pp. 46-47.
5. William McKinney, "Revisioning the Future of Old Line Protestantism," *The Christian Century* (8 November 1989); p. 1016.

HOW SHALL
WE PREACH?

Thomas H. Troeger

CAN YOU IMAGINE THIS?

THE FUTURE ROLE OF IMAGINATION IN PREACHING

Can you imagine this?

> *I've got a robe, you've got a robe,*
> *All of God's children got a robe.*
> *When I get to heaven goin' to put on my robe,*
> *Goin' to shout all over God's heav'n.*
> *Heav'n, heav'n,*
> *Ev'rybody talkin' bout heav'n ain't goin' there*
> *Heav'n, heav'n,*
> *Goin' to shout all over God's heav'n.*[1]

Can you imagine this? Not just as your isolated self reading these words, but can you imagine this as the slave who is being sold in the following account of a slave auction market?

> Beside [the slave auctioneer] is a man with black skin, and clothed in rough garments. His looks are downcast and submissive. He is being sold, just like a horse at Tattersall's or a picture at Christie

135

and Manson's—I must be under some illusion. That dark object, whom I have been always taught to consider a man, is not a man."[2]

This is a description of hell. For hell is wherever human beings treat others "like a horse . . . or a picture," denying their value, refusing to recognize that they too are made in the image of God.

Can you imagine this? The question is far more than an exercise of fantasy. It has been a matter of survival. When you are in hell, it takes a courageous act of religious imagination to affirm your value, and that is exactly what African American preachers have helped their people do, generation after generation. Although these preachers have been gifted individuals, their spiritual genius has been fed by the larger imagination of the entire community. This was the case from the beginning as African slaves worked to develop a system of religious meaning and support to counter the brutality of their servitude:

> Africans were creative in Africa; they did not cease to be creative as involuntary settlers in America. . . . The story of the emergence of African-American Christianity is a story of an emergent African-American culture as well as of residual African cultures, a story of innovation as well as of tradition, a story of change as well as continuity.[3]

This larger cultural context reminds us that the work of the homiletical imagination is rooted in and intertwined with the imagination of the community. Understood from this perspective, imagination is more than the act of "forming a mental concept of what is not actually present to the senses."[4] Imagination is the visionary work of a culture that creates a universe of stories, images, and rituals to sustain its life by giving hope and meaning to people.

Imagination as the creative work of a culture is more like a tree than a cloud. To be an imaginative preacher does not mean waiting for a cloud to appear in the sky of your mind. Instead, you graft your creativity to the richly rooted, thickly branched tree that has been cultivated by the entire community, that tree that is its heritage, its tradition of song and prayer, praise and proclamation, survival and resistance.

We can learn how to do this from those Black preachers who helped their people survive by building up a vision of their dignity as human beings and feeding their dreams of freedom. The role of imagination in their preaching points to the future role of imagination in all preaching. We will use imagination to present a vision that empowers our communities to continue the just and compassionate ministry of Jesus.

Although many churches and racial groups have participated in this ministry, I believe African American traditions have a special contribution to make because the imaginative work of African American religious leaders has been refined and tested in the crucible of centuries of suffering and injustice. The spirit of the one who has promised to be among the least of humanity permeates their homiletical imagination. And yet, as Henry Mitchell has long affirmed, the insights of Black preaching traditions are not for African American preachers alone. They have much wider significance," reaching across our human divisions.[5]

As a White preacher and homiletician, I owe an incalculable debt to African American preachers and scholars who have taught me about the faithful use of the imagination in the proclamation of the gospel.[6] These learnings operate simultaneously at a theological and a practical level, instructing me in both the meaning and the methods of preaching imaginatively. This fusion of theology and practice, meaning and method, reminds us that the imaginative work of African American Christianity is not merely adornment or subterfuge. There is a depth in its lack of embellishment, a wisdom in its poetry. We can see it in the spiritual that I quoted earlier. Upon first reading or singing, the words are charming and seemingly naive. But when one considers the line "Ev'rybody talkin' 'bout heav'n ain't goin' there" in the context of slavery, then it becomes apparent that a vision of justice has been compressed into a phrase, a lyric that the oppressors may think harmless, while in truth it is working to subvert their power. Like many spirituals and much Black preaching, the song serves both to comfort people who are suffering and to motivate these people to continue striving for justice. In his book *Wade in the Water*, Arthur C. Jones writes, "the almost unbearable suffering of the present was at times made more bearable by the ability to imagine a better life beyond death, which in turn helped provide the necessary energy to engage in the struggle to hasten the time of earthly freedom."[7]

To create words customary but profound, soothing yet empowering, whether in spiritual or sermon, requires an act of *sophisticated imagining*. How will preachers continue the faithful use of the imagination into the future? I believe there are principles, ways of perceiving and responding to our life situation, that foster such imaginative homiletical work, and these principles can help us in claiming the future role of imagination in preaching. In what follows I name some of these principles, pairing each principle with a Black spiritual in order to capture the poetic and affective dimensions without which the principle is paralyzed. I draw upon these musical, poetic resources because the witness of the Black church and nearly all the scholarship I have read about its practices demonstrate the insoluble bonds between music and preaching, the way one often flows into the other.

A Theology of Sovereignty, an Anthropology of Wholeness

"I'm gonna sing when the Spirit says sing."

The poet gives us a theology and an anthropology. It is a theology that posits the initiative and freedom of a sovereign God. We sing or shout or preach or pray, not "when we feel like it," but when "the Spirit says." And this theology is complemented by an anthropology of the whole person. The different verbs of successive stanzas employ various aspects of our humanity: our voices ("sing"), our minds and hearts ("preach"), our bodies ("dance and shout"). Our whole being is open to the Spirit. To engage all that we are in praise of God is a way of affirming our created goodness. Such affirmation serves as a bulwark against the tide of negative messages sent by our culture. The spiritual makes it clear that every aspect of our humanity is worthy of being used to glorify God. But at the same time this affirmation of our created selves is not allowed to lead to arrogance. For all of these gifts are placed at the service of the Spirit. To sing and to preach such a theology and anthropology is a liberating act, and the slaves must have known this with a special poignance. In their daily life they had to do what their masters said or face horrible consequences. But in their souls they knew that the only one they would ever freely obey was the sovereign Spirit of God.

Here then is a practical, theological way to develop our homiletical imagination: *expand the number of ways we prepare for a sermon*. Instead of limiting it to the process of our thought, we can spend time listening for what the Spirit says. Respond as the Spirit directs—sing, pray, dance, mime—and see what happens with our homiletical imagination.

Fearless Invocation

"I want Jesus to walk with me."

One of the greatest barriers to receiving the Holy Spirit through the work of the imagination is the biblicism that braids the language of Scripture into a rope for making a noose. The slaves suffered under such biblicism because it was one of the tools their oppressors used to sanctify and condone their evil.[8] The slaves deconstructed this authoritarian literalism by being biblical without becoming biblicist; that is to say, the slaves honored the spirit and the living presence of Jesus without turning the Bible into an idol. Thus a slave explained her understanding of the gospel by responding: "I can't read a word. But I read Jesus in my heart. . . . I knows he's there 'cause I read him in my heart, just like you know about him from reading the book!"[9] The woman understands that Jesus did not say, "Follow a text," but "Follow me." She cuts the noose of literalism and appeals directly to her living savior.

Again and again in the record of Black song and sermon, we see this fearless invocation of the divine, a boldness that blends reverence with intimacy in calling upon holy powers:

> I want Jesus to walk with me;
> I want Jesus to walk with me;
> All along my pilgrim journey, Lord,
> I want Jesus to walk with me.

Here then is a practical, theological, spiritual way to develop our homiletical imagination: *read Jesus in our hearts and mark what we learn from Jesus there*. Then sing the spiritual, and ask where we have to walk on that pilgrim journey. In what valley? To what mountain? Through what wilderness? Over what river? We will not hold back our needs from God. What do we need to survive, to reach the promised land?

Our need is as real as our congregation's, and we will not be able to give a bold witness to God on their behalf unless we fearlessly invoke the divine on our own behalf.

Utter Realism

"Nobody knows the trouble I see, Glory, hallelujah!"

Common speech often distinguishes between reality and what is only imagined. We say of an illusion, "It's just in your imagination." But in fact there is a reciprocal dialogue between reality and imagination in the creating of who we are, not only as individuals, but as a society. Thus, for example, at the core of America's self-understanding are two radically different imaginings of who we are as a nation.

Of course, there are really far more than two, but for now we will consider the two American self-understandings that are perhaps the most polarized and defining. Albert J. Raboteau, in his essay "African Americans, Exodus and the American Israel," delineates them well:

> From the earliest days of colonization, white Christians had represented their journey across the Atlantic to America as the exodus of a New Israel from the bondage of Egypt into the Promised Land of milk and honey. For black Christians, the imagery was reversed: the Middle Passage had brought them to Egypt land, where they suffered bondage under a new Pharaoh. White Christians saw themselves as the New Israel; slaves identified themselves as the Old. This is, as Vincent Harding remarked, one of the abiding and tragic ironies of our history: the nation's claim to be the New Israel was contradicted by the Old Israel still enslaved in her midst.[10]

Raboteau ends his essay with a single potent question: "Is America Israel, or is she Egypt?[11] The question compels us to face what understanding of America rules the airwaves, the political decisions, the definition of morality and family values. The witness of Black preaching and worship is that facing up to the Egypt in our national character—the enslaving and oppressive realities of our society—is a beginning point for any act of homiletical imagination that will feed authentic redemption.

Henry Mitchell sees such realism as an essential part of what he terms the "celebration" that marks Black preaching (and that can mark all preaching):

> It couples a realistic facing of the hardest aspects of existence with a firm determination to fix consciousness on whatsoever things exist for which there can be praise to God. The Spiritual puts it, Nobody knows the trouble I see, Glory Hallelujah![12]

Here, then, is a practical, theological, spiritual way to develop one's homiletical imagination: *name the trouble you see, the cruel wrong*. Look it in the eye. Describe it as it is, and then end our description not with a period, but a comma, "Nobody knows the trouble I see," and hold that comma like a fermata in a piece of music, like a prayer too deep for words, one that our groanings give over to the Spirit, for only she can utter such language. Hold it until we find the place where "Glory Hallelujah!" breaks in. Let the juxtaposition of trouble and Hallelujah be what Paul Scott Wilson compares to the spark gap between two charged wires,[13] the place where imagination leaps to find connections of grace and meaning that otherwise would never occur.

A Community of Liberty

"Let us break bread together on our knees."

The word *bread* often symbolizes, in African American services, the Word of God, as in the preacher who is "to break the bread [Word] of life." Without for a moment lessening the importance of this spiritual to the celebration of the Lord's Supper, I want to consider what it suggests about increasing the imaginative capacity of preachers.

"Let us break bread together on our knees." Note four things about that opening line. It does not depend on the preacher alone, but on the gathered community. Secondly, we are expecting to be fed. Preaching is serving up a meal for hungry folk. Third, the bread has to be broken. You cannot eat the whole loaf at once! And finally, we are going to do this on our knees, the preacher along with everyone else. We all recognize our dependence upon the generous host.

The accumulative effect of these various elements is the building up of a community where liberty is experienced in multiple dimensions by the entire group. Thus Donald G. Matthews writes about worship in slave communities:

> The word sometimes used to describe the feelings released in worship was "liberty". The connotations are clear—liberation from the fear of death, apprehension about the future, guilt for having done those things one ought not to have done, shame for not having done those things one ought to have done; liberation, too, from the masters. Liberty was an expression of relief . . . and the joy of realizing what one's humanity meant. It was expressed in communal dance, song, and open approval of the preacher's words: "Yes, oh yes!" "Amen!" "That's right—Amen!" In the communal celebration of the Spirit of God was the celebration that the Spirit knew neither rank nor race, and no condition of servitude; it was celebration of human equality—"God is no respecter of persons."[14]

Here, then, is a practical, theological, spiritual way to develop our homiletical imagination: *reconfigure the way we imagine ourselves before the congregation.* Even if we will be standing in the pulpit when we preach, we cannot start our homiletical imaginings there. We will start on our knees with the community gathered around us. What are we hungering for as a member of the community? How is our hunger shared by the others? How will we and the congregation break the bread together?

Counter Imagination

"All of God's children got shoes."

I close with another verse from the spiritual with which we opened. It reminds us that a central goal of all this homiletical imagining is to picture the world as God intends it to be. A foreign observer at a church service in the antebellum South reported that of the slaves in attendance "About one-half of them had shoes on."[15] Think of those calloused feet standing in scalding fields in the heat of summer, think of the chill up through the legs when the frost came. And yet the slaves sang, "All of God's children got shoes." Their imagination was a counter imagination, a God-given capacity to envision the world as it is meant to be, a power of soul greater than the power of their masters.

Here, then, is a practical, theological, spiritual way to develop our homiletical imagination: *counter the world that is with a vision of the world that God is empowering us to create, and preach and work to bring that world to be.* For that is the true work of the faithful imagination.

Henry Mitchell provides us with insightful advice, as he talks about how African slaves survived in America without losing their sanity, despite the barbaric treatment they endured: "They took the initiative to choose their internal living space. With a genius for psychic survival, if there was *any* praise, they thought on these things."[16]

Can you imagine this? Learning from our great African American preaching tradition how we preachers can choose our internal living space (the home of our imaginations) by choosing to think in a way that would give God the praise, by the principles of utter realism, fearless invocation, communities of liberty, a theology of sovereignty, an anthropology of wholeness, and acts of counter imagination. If we can imagine this, then we are on our way to understanding the future role of imagination in preaching.

NOTES

1. All quotations of spirituals are from *Songs of Zion: Supplemental Worship Resources 12* (Nashville: Abingdon Press, 1981). I am deeply indebted in my discussion of this spiritual and all that follow to Arthur C. Jones, *Wade in the Water: The Wisdom of the Spirituals* (Maryknoll, N.Y.: Orbis Books, 1993).
2. William Chambers, *Things As They Are in America* (Philadelphia: Lippincott, Grambo, & Co., 1854), pp. 269-86, quoted in *A Documentary History of Slavery in North America*, ed. Willie Lee Rose (New York: Oxford University Press, 1976), p. 150.
3. Charles Joyner, " 'Believer I Know': The Emergence of African American Christianity," in *African American Christianity: Essays in History*, ed. Paul E. Johnson (Berkeley: University of California Press, 1994), p. 19.
4. *The Compact Oxford English Dictionary*, second edition (New York: Oxford University Press, 1987).
5. Henry H. Mitchell, *The Recovery of Preaching* (San Francisco: Harper & Row, 1977), p. 12.
6. In addition to Henry H. Mitchell, who has taught me through his writings, lectures, and sermons, I think especially of Evans Crawford, James Forbes, Teresa Fry, Vincent Harding, Toinette Eugene, Brenda Hazel, James Earl Massey, Ella Pearson Mitchell, Gardner Taylor, Linda Thomas, Gayraud Willmore, members of the East Denver Alliance, and dozens of African American students who have been in my preaching courses. Their voices, faith, and thoughts are helping me write this article in ways too numerous to cite.
7. Jones, *Wade in the Water*, p. 88.
8. See for example Howell Cobb, *A Scriptural Examination of the Institution of Slavery in the United States; with Its Objects and Purposes*, 1856, a polemic for slavery, based on the Bible.

9. Quoted in Melva Wilson Costen, *African American Christian Worship* (Nashville: Abingdon Press, 1993), p. 21.
10. Albert J. Raboteau, "African Americans, Exodus and the American Israel," in *African American Christianity: Essays in History*, ed. Paul E. Johnson (Berkeley: University of California Press, 1994), p. 9.
11. Raboteau, "African Americans, Exodus and the American Israel," p. 15.
12. Mitchell, *The Recovery of Preaching*, p. 57.
13. Paul Scott Wilson, *Imagination of the Heart: New Understandings in Preaching* (Nashville: Abingdon Press, 1988).
14. Donald G. Matthews, "Religion and Slavery—The Case of the American South," in *Anti-Slavery, Religion and Reform: Essays in Memory of Roger Anstey*, eds. Christine Bolt, Seymour Drescher, (Hamden, Conn.: Archon Books, 1980), p. 227.
15. William Thomson, *A Tradesman's Travels, in the United States and Canada* (Edinburgh: Oliver & Boyd, 1842), quoted in *A Documentary History of Slavery in North America*, ed. Willie Lee Rose, p. 465.
16. Mitchell, *The Recovery of Preaching*, p. 48.

CHAPTER THIRTEEN

Edwina Hunter

FINALLY SAID: WOMEN MUST PREACH DIFFERENTLY THAN MEN

*W*hy *are so many women responding to a vocational* call to ministry—all types of ministry, and especially preaching minis- try? We know women affirming a "call to preach" is a phenomenon of the past two decades that arguably cannot be matched in history. From my position, as a subjective participant and observer, I am forced to conclude that there must be a reason or reasons beyond those we have previously acknowledged.

I have been preaching and teaching preaching for almost twenty years. The questions I raise here have been with me for a long while. More than a decade ago, on a grant from the Association of Theologi- cal Schools, I visited seminaries, selected for their theological and cultural diversity, to question professors of preaching about two things: (1) their methodology for teaching diverse cultures, including men, women, gays, lesbians, and persons of various ethnic origins, in the same course; (2) their expert "take" on how women students were performing in their classes in comparison with men students. With this second line of questioning, I wanted to know if they perceived any gender differences in preaching.

Are there gender differences in preaching? For years teaching both men and women students in class together, I have wanted to say, indeed have said, that there are really no gender differences; rather each student must seek to find his or her own voice for preaching. However, increasingly over the last few years, my attitude has definitely changed. I continue trying to provide an atmosphere in which men and women can discover for themselves their own individual preaching voices; yet I cannot help being aware of how many differences there are between the acculturation of women and of men, as well as psychological and physiological differences. I have had years now to observe closely some radical differences in the interpretation of a given scripture text. Therefore, I now ask myself the same question I once asked my colleagues around the country.

Are there gender differences in preaching? I do not know. I only know that something deep inside me demands a speaking out: *If there are no gender differences in preaching, then there should be!* I tell students in preaching classes never to use such words as "should" in sermons except on exceedingly rare occasions. Yet, I declare that there *should* be gender differences in preaching because I have come to believe that the One in whose name we preach has a purpose beyond our imagining. Why call so many women to a preaching vocation if women are not going to be different from men in their preaching? Why call so many women if they are not going to say things that men have not said or do not say? Why call women to preach if they do not speak in ways strangely yet surely integral to the wholeness of being women?

Therefore, my purpose here is not to establish, once and for all, that there are gender differences in preaching, but simply to declare that there should be. And closely related to that, my purpose is to urge each woman preacher to join me in a conscious quest to discover who you are, what you are to say, how you are to say it, and ultimately, to seek to answer for yourself, why has God called you, a woman, to preach?

Who Am I?

Who are you? Who am I? You are a woman and I am a woman and we live among, relate to and connect with many other women. Yet, the *we* of women is not monolithic. However much we identify our individual selves, as womanists, as feminists, as mujueristas, among others who identify themselves in the same manner, each of us is engaged in the process of discovering who is the one named I.

We enter the journey to the I of who we are at different points. We follow the journey along different paths, often asking very different questions. Yet it is vital for us to realize that no matter how alone we sometimes feel, or how much a stranger, most of us do seek relationship and common ground upon which to share our stories. We seek companions and those who will listen us into wholeness. More often than not, we find those we seek among women who are also seeking relationship, common ground, wholeness. We discover that we learn from each other, that we receive gifts of stories and poems, tears and laughter, that together, we grow in our understanding of whom we are and whom the One is calling us to be. There are times when we know for ourselves that we find love along the way and that "the journey is home" as Nellie Morton so poignantly documented.[1] At other times, we know that we do not know how to love ourselves, and if we do not know how to love ourselves as *woman*, then how can we possibly discover ourselves as *preacher*?

What do we need to recall, to re-member, in order to know ourselves and claim all of who we are? We need to release our memories, and in doing so, discover those persons and experiences that shaped us. The release of memories may reveal, in some of us, wounds inflicted by the scorching disapproval of those in power. Others will discover deep scars that ache when a cold wind of rejection comes blowing around us. After all, we have known rejection before. Who we are is the sum total of all of our life experiences, of all the people with whom we have interacted, of all our mistakes, and our accomplishments. So tell your stories to others, especially to other women, and let them offer in return their own stories. Listen one another into healing and possibility.

Please hear me. The pain and the joy, the tears and the laughter are the very stuff of preaching. We are who we are because of everything that has ever happened to us. God's grace works to help us move toward wholeness and integration. All the time, we are becoming who each of us is, a woman among women whom we love and with whom we identify. Each of us is becoming a woman preacher or a preacher woman, free to preach the gospel of liberating love and acceptance for all to hear. The reality is that, as Dr. James Forbes says in a powerful sermon on Joseph, "When the GREAT I AM tells me who I am, then I can tell anyone WHO I AM."

Therefore, I ask you to ask God, "Who am I?" Wait for God's answer. Wait until that answer rises within you as burning as the call of Moses, as awesome as the call of Isaiah, as dreadful as the call of Jeremiah, as inevitable as the call of Mary to give birth to Jesus, and as profound as the call of Mary Magdalene to bear witness to the resurrection of the Christ. After the waiting, I ask you, "Who are you?" I hear you reply, "I am Woman. I am Preacher. I am who *I am*."

What Do I Preach?

Dr. Ella Mitchell first gave to a coterie of African American women preachers the designation of "preaching women."[2] We are becoming aware that there are women in every culture and race in our country who are called, named, and chosen to be preaching women. What do we preach? Just as women are not all the same, neither are we all called to preach the same message. The One who calls knows we seek common ground and companionship and unity; however, that One also knows that our differences give opportunity for the gospel message to emerge in many diverse voices and languages. Thus, I ask, "What do I preach?"

This is where we get into deep water. If my hypothesis holds, that the One who calls is calling so many women because we are indeed to speak what men do not speak, then this is the point at which we have to get serious. We need to learn or invent methods of discovery. We need to learn ways of listening to each other and to our congregations. We need to draw on our own unique value as woman. We need to study and do deep reading of the Scriptures, and of books by women scholars that help us read with a woman's eyes. Ultimately, we need to immerse ourselves, our souls and psyches and bodies, in the stories, geography, and writings of women from cultures other than our own, as well as from our own. We need to discover in persons and in books how we relate to one another across cultural and racial lines. We need to know what the One who calls wants us to speak concerning the centuries of oppression, poverty, and pain endured, and still endured, by women and children of every color.

Nor are we excused from hearing the stories of our brothers of whatever race or culture. But we need not overly concern ourselves with making an effort to hear our brothers' stories: society will ensure this. The call to preach justice may well be discerned in our own individual experience of injustice; however, until we open our eyes to the injustice experienced by every part of humanity, we have not fully responded, "Here I am, Holy One, send me." However, for the purposes of this brief essay, please let me concentrate on the ways in which women learn what to preach.

I want to begin with discoveries of women scholars and the affirmation that they can help us read the Scriptures with a woman's eyes. What is it that they are telling us? They are unequivocal in their insistence that Christian womanists, feminists, and mujueristas, as well as those of us who identify ourselves simply as women, are being asked to join with the struggle of oppressed women and children everywhere. A primary challenge comes in the manner in which we read the Bible itself.

Reading the Bible with Woman's Eyes

Professor Delores Williams provides one of the clearest proposals I have read about how womanist preachers can preach the Bible with a different perspective from that of African American male preachers.

> Black Liberation theology is providing the theological explication of the liberation principle of black biblical interpretation. Womanist survivalist/quality-of-life theology (at least in this book) is beginning to provide the theological explication of the survival principle of African American biblical interpretation. When our hermeneutical principle is God's word of survival and quality of life to oppressed communities (or families) living in a Diaspora, we put different emphasis upon biblical texts and identify with different biblical stories than do black liberation theologians.[3]

Williams acknowledges that some "womanist theologians are more committed to the liberation hermeneutic while other womanist theologians may be more committed to the survival/quality-of-life hermeneutic." She suggests dialogue between the two groups and further suggests that "Hispanic feminist theologians and some Jewish feminist theologians, who understand survival to be a primary issue in their communities might also join this dialogue."[4] Clearly, a woman learns much in dialogue with other women about what she is to preach and what hermeneutic will enable her to find her own voice for preaching.

Women of any culture who desire to know more about how Hispanic women find their voices are advised to read the book *Hispanic Women: Prophetic Voice in the Church*, by Ada Maria Isasi-Diaz and Yolanda Tarango.[5] The relationship to the Bible of these Hispanic women is markedly different from that of feminist or womanist theologians. Conversation among us is important.

Feminist biblical interpretation has burgeoned in recent years. Any woman seeking to find her own voice for preaching will want to read the works of Elisabeth Schüssler Fiorenza, especially *Searching the Scriptures: A Feminist Introduction*. The questions raised in this book are, "Do women and men read the Scriptures differently? Do they bring different concerns and presuppositions to the text? use different methods? read with 'different eyes'? and should they?"[6] These questions are closely akin to the ones with which I began. My answer, from long experience in hearing men and women preach in the same classes, is a resounding YES! Each woman preacher who keenly desires to discover what God would have her preach must learn to read the Bible with different eyes.

Different eyes can be opened quite rapidly with the reading of Phyllis Trible's *Texts of Terror*. Trible brings wide-open eyes to interpretations of four narratives from the Hebrew Scriptures.[7] I advise that the one who has never opened the pages of this book not do so just before bedtime. Sleep may be long in coming.

Another book that can be eye-opening, and perhaps ensure that women can never preach without being aware of their gender as a major factor in claiming their voices, is *Just a Sister Away: A Womanist Vision of Women's Relationships in the Bible*, by Renita J. Weems.[8] This book deals with some of the stories that are treated in Trible's work. Weems speaks from a strong womanist stance that will help the reader realize the need for women to dialogue and read across cultural and racial lines.

What do we preach? We preach the Bible, but not as the Bible has ever been preached before. We find our individual and unique woman's voice and woman's response. Reading these books I have suggested will help, and so will listening to one another's stories. The stories of biblical women, the stories of women from history, and the stories of contemporary women need to be heard and told by women. Women can tell stories that acknowledge injustice and pain and that also bring healing and a sense of solidarity where only alienation had been present. What do we preach? We preach what we discern the One who called us wants us to preach.

How Do We Preach?

Who are we, what do we preach, *how do we preach?* Let me ask another question: How do you live? What is most important to you in your life? What makes up the very fabric of your existence? Let me answer for myself: Relationships. Relationships—deep, interactive, at times intimate relationships—are the primary stuff of my joys and sorrows and of how I live. Many women have said that this is also true for them. If it is so for you, then I ask you, "How do you preach?" You answer, "I preach relationally."

What does it mean to preach relationally? I think it means that we enter into an in-depth relationship with the scripture text through prayer, imagination, living with the scripture, carrying it around with us until a personal story emerges that helps our herstory and the scripture to intersect. We come into a sense of ownership of the text.

Next, we enter into a relationship with the people among whom we preach. As Henry Mitchell has often said, we attempt to sit where the people sit. And more than that, we listen to them as they talk and even when they do not talk. We carry them around in our hearts and imaginations. Imaginatively, we let them ask us questions about the text, about life, about their own concerns; and, imaginatively, we dialogue with them as we prepare to preach. We pray for these people. If possible, we go into the space where they and we will be for worship and the sermon. We stand where we will stand to preach and we look out and remember where individuals and families sit. In our imaginations, we see them, and we pray for them. We love them. We consciously love them. Then, when we stand in that same space actually to preach, we let our voices, our facial expressions, our gestures, our love reach out clearly to these people rationally. We preach among them, at times for them as their spokesperson, yet as one of them.

We discover that we must also be in close relationship, simultaneously, with ourselves and with the One who called us. That relationship can bring about what we call incarnational preaching. We embody the Word. We let the gospel live through us and in us. Our bodies come alive and we tell the story we preach with our whole beings, from the tops of our heads through the soles our feet. *How do we preach? Relationally and incarnationally.*

In conclusion, I offer the words written by Prathia Hall Wynn in the foreword of *Those Preachin' Women*:

> The proclaimers [in this book] are unapologetically Black women preachers. Their identity is grounded in the intrinsic dynamic of each of these realities. Their messages are forged in the crucible of their experience of blackness, femaleness, and the liberation of God in Jesus Christ. Their response to the call of God has often been the product of protracted struggle. Yet when the "yes" finally ushered from the center of their being, they knew that it had been there all the time and that before they were even formed in the womb they were called and anointed. Like Jeremiah they learned that to refuse to preach is to experience a fire in one's bones that can be quenched by nothing less than faithful, obedient preaching.[9]

What do these words mean for all of us, whoever we are? I think they mean that each of us must discover her own identity, who she is. Then, they mean that we discover what crucible has forged our particular message. We learn what we are to preach. And, third, they mean that each one of us will preach with the power of the Spirit, of imagination, of passion, of conviction, relationally and incarnationally releasing the fire in her own bones. This is what it means to be called, a woman, to preach.

NOTES

1. Nell Morton, *The Journey Is Home* (Boston: Beacon Press, 1985). See especially "1970: Women—On the March"; "1971: The Rising Woman Consciousness in a Male Language Structure"; "1976: Educating for Wholeness."

2. See two books edited by Ella Pearson Mitchell: *Those Preachin' Women: Sermons by Black Women Preachers* (Valley Forge: Judson Press, 1985) and *Those Preaching Women: More Sermons by Black Women Preachers* (Valley Forge: Judson Press, 1989).

3. Delores S. Williams, *Sisters in the Wilderness: The Challenge of Womanist God-Talk* (Maryknoll, N.Y.: Orbis Books, 1993), p. 193.

4. Ibid., p. 194.

5. Ada Maria Isasi-Diaz and Yolanda Tarango, *Hispanic Women: Prophetic Voice in the Church* (San Francisco: Harper & Row, 1988).

6. See the dust cover of Elisabeth Schüssler Fiorenza, ed., *Searching the Scriptures, Volume I: A Feminist Introduction* (New York: Crossroad, 1993.) Also see other books by Schüssler Fiorenza: *But She Said* (Boston: Beacon Press, 1992); *In Memory of Her* (New York: Crossroad, 1985); *Bread Not Stone* (Boston: Beacon Press, 1984).

7. Phyllis Trible, *Texts of Terror: Literary-Feminist Readings of Biblical Narratives* (Philadelphia: Fortress Press, 1984).

8. Renita J. Weems, *Just A Sister Away: A Womanist Vision of Women's Relationships in the Bible* (San Diego: LuraMedia, 1988).

9. Ella Pearson Mitchell, ed., *Those Preachin' Women*, pp. 9-10.

CHAPTER FOURTEEN

Samuel D. Proctor

P R O P H E T I C

P R E A C H I N G

N O W

A GENERATION AFTER KING

*T*he Black community learned early how to find its strength and inspiration by transcending its immediate, historical situation, and learning how to live in lofty places. The faith of Black people delivered them from their oppression and wafted their souls into realms eternal. And the one who led them in this experience was the preacher, the one called to stand between their travail and their God.

That preacher has been the object of caricature and ridicule, the subject of minstrel and Broadway shows, and the target of a catalogue of jokes. Yet, generation after generation, it was to that much distorted personality that the souls of Black folk turned to learn of their deliverance. This preacher and his or her role have been incomparably described in all of their shades and tones in the writings of Dr. Henry Mitchell.

Perhaps the high moment for Black preaching was reached during that pinnacle of Black striving, the Civil Rights movement. While Martin Luther King Jr. became the epitome of this movement, all over the country Black preachers were on the wall crying out for justice—in Los Angeles, Detroit, Brooklyn, Philadelphia, Boston, Houston, Birmingham, Baltimore, and Richmond. Even in rural areas the Black preacher kept the issue of justice alive. Indeed, many were silent, passive and acquiescent, but the changes wrought were won by the constant agitation of Blacks in their communities with preachers on the front line.

Easily, it is conceded that these preachers had the advantage of being independent and generally beyond reprisal. Their institution was owned and controlled by their own people; and hardly any other Black had the freedom to represent the claims and the frustrations of Blacks like the preacher.

Black Americans are entirely unique in the history of the world. We started out 4 million strong, at our emancipation from slavery in 1863, with no education, no money, no property, and burdened with a stigma imposed by the dehumanization of 244 years of chattel slavery.

Here we are in 1995: over forty of us are in Congress; six are in the presidential Cabinet; one has been chairman of the joint chiefs of staff; one is America's poet laureate; one heads the largest philanthropy in the world; one heads the largest pension plan in the world; one has been the manager of a major league baseball team that won the World Series championship two years back-to-back. And our perseverance has been due largely to the role and function of the preacher.

But also today, after the gains of the sixties, we have had the presidencies of Nixon, Reagan, and Bush, and the rise of the Christian Right. We have seen the slow but certain growth of reaction against people of color, against the poor, against liberals, which reached a climax in 1994 with these forces gaining control of Congress. The principal consequences have been a slowdown of our ultimate liberation and the stagnation of a large, growing Black underclass. It is a class that is poorly educated, lacking in self-esteem, and jobless. Many are on public assistance, many are teenage parents, and from them has come a steady procession of young Black males headed for crime and jail. This dysfunctional underclass is further victimized by the drug scourge.

One could start at many points in addressing this, but just as the Black preacher pioneered and led us out of the morass of segregation, now we need the same prophetic preaching to dismantle this matrix of social, moral, and spiritual failure. We need prophets to proclaim the Word of the Lord now, in the present crisis, to undo this awful state of affairs. Getting started on this is our priority. How?

1. Such a prophetic preacher must first call our Black communities to restore our original quest for racial uplift from within, emphasizing ethnic pride and resourcefulness.

Strange, this is what our enemies say too, but the fact is that we never needed anyone else to remind us of the need for dignity and self-reliance. Where on earth would we be if we had not lived by this creed? We do have too many young men displaying unsociable behavior, and we do have too many children having children, but these are not the main flow of Black life.

All Black colleges are filled to overflowing; we are increasing our numbers in the traditionally White institutions; and every morning the masses of Black folk are at work somewhere. But those interested in our demise would have us think differently. When the media reports that 30 percent of our girls under sixteen are having babies, why don't they tell us what the other 70 percent are doing? When they tell us that 25 percent of our young men ages eighteen to thirty-five are incarcerated, why don't they tell us about the 75 percent who are not? Yet we do know what our failures are and considering what we have endured no one knows how many more failures we might have had.

Nevertheless, we need our preachers to rise up and call those who have given up to stir up their pride and respect. Much of this must be a call to discipline and hard effort, to sacrifice and devotion. And sadly, too many of our preachers are not calling our people to discipline and devotion. They are preaching a soft message of materialism and selfish regard. Services are dominated by the theme of what God gives us, not what we give in service and devotion. It is a gospel of *"give me"* and not a message of *"use me."* It is all "Thank you Jesus," and "Thank you Lord for what you have done for me." God is a cosmic bellhop. In many services nothing else is said or sung except about what God can do for us! This is not prophetic preaching; it is barely preaching at all. We have gone far in cultivating a religion about Jesus—his salvific work on the cross and in the resurrection, and the sacerdotal efficacy of the Eucharist. But we have done this at the expense of discipleship: following Jesus. It has been far more attractive to celebrate Jesus as Savior than to follow him as Master; to wear his cross as jewelry than to bear his cross as a habit of the heart. Instead of bearing the old rugged cross, we have painted it gold and hung it around our necks, deluding ourselves that someone will see and believe that we are Christians.

The corollary is that, sadly, the preacher too often tries to show how good God is by the preacher's own extravagant dress, excessive jewelry, self-aggrandizing gestures, expensive cars, and exhibitionist residences. Religion has gone Hollywood—commercial, sensate, materialistic, and vulgar.

We need new prophets who love Jesus rather than themselves. We need persons whose own lives bear the marks of discipleship, and who can therefore be authentic in calling others to self-love, respect, and Christian discipline and devotion.

2. Next, prophetic preaching will have to reach deeper than the culpability of those who are victims of oppression themselves, and probe the political order that protects and perpetuates the status quo.

Indeed, those who have lost their way do need us to call them to self-love, self-help, and racial uplift, but any solid reading of history and understanding in our society will show how structured and systemic the economic order is and how it is intertwined with the political order, which directly impacts the social order. Recently it was reported that the poorest counties in South Carolina have the worst pollution of air, rivers, and streams by toxic industrial waste in the nation. Major corporations move to South Carolina because its pollution laws are so lax. A Virginia Congressman has pledged that no anti-tobacco legislation will get through the committee that he chairs. Politics and money!

If the prophetic preachers keep such matters exposed to public light, a new political consensus can be built. After all, there was a time when women could not vote and Social Security and Medicare were called communistic.

Whenever it is election time, we know that the politicians will be seeking comment from the pulpit. They will be seeking endorsements. It seems now that many preachers are so eager to be partners with politicians and to be chosen for political favors that they are rendered impotent in challenging the politics of oppression.

The new prophet must be free to call any party, any candidate, any public official to accountability. The new prophet cannot be so tied up by political favors, grants, and appointments as to be rendered speechless. If Nathan had been wining and dining with David, he could never have challenged David for having Uriah killed and taking Uriah's wife! But thank God, Nathan was free.

Another significant aspect of the role of the new prophet is to learn the vocabulary of politics, the numbers of politics, the history and personalities of politics, and the efficacy of political engagement to keep his or her people alert to enemies.

Some of the most inspiring reading I have found are the pages of Dr. Edward Wheeler's book *Racial Uplift*,[2] in which he describes the rhetoric and the labors of Black preachers during the first thirty years following slavery. The Black preachers rolled like thunder to keep their people politically alert. J. C. Price and Henry McNeal Turner were shining examples of political acumen. Some of them accepted public office, but they are best remembered for their oratory of commitment to the struggles of their people. Every aspect of life is political. The plight of the poor is political, awaiting a prophet to unravel it for the people—a prophet who will train and empower the masses so that they can stand up and participate in the shaping of their own destiny.

3. As we take an even closer look at the condition of those who are left out, left behind, and left alone in our society, these challenges—moral, economic, and social—are only a prelude to what it will take to break the bonds of poverty and isolation.

The Internal Revenue Service would admit that a large percent of their returns come from persons earning $50,000 or less. Then there is that 9 percent who control most of the earnings in America. The head of the Coca-Cola Corporation makes $40,000 an hour. Michael Jordan is paid $235,000 a game, and some big-name university basketball coaches' yearly salaries run into six figures. The income gap between the executives and the workers in our country is much wider than that of other industrialized nations. And there is no national debate on these matters. Years ago the only response to this situation was socialism, government ownership of production and distribution of goods and services. And the clear criticism of that approach was that sin and greed, malfeasance, and hanky-panky could corrupt any system.

Since we say that we choose to have a democracy, we should behave like a democracy. In this so-called democracy we have all of the instruments that we need to save us from this vulgar disparity in our society. Now all we need are prophets with godly wills and godly courage. Free people, with prophetic leadership, can achieve a new conscience, a new conviction on matters; and our present *institutions* can change!

During the Reagan years it became respectable to blame the poor for their poverty, to condemn those who needed help from the government, and to cut in half the tax on super incomes. The tax rate for the very rich fell dramatically. The national debt grew astronomically, and now welfare recipients and illegal aliens are blamed for the debt.

Many preachers have adopted a sickening, vulgar, materialistic lifestyle that has confused laypersons and further disillusioned the unchurched. Such preachers have invented a Christ who bears no resemblance to the historic Jesus. Meanwhile, the chronic condition of the poor remains unchallenged. Such preachers are themselves like the members of the leisure class; they imitate the lifestyle of the well-to-do, and the poor are regarded as losers, a kind of caste that inevitably belongs in every society. The very poor, therefore, have no real advocates.

Jesus was disturbed by the plight of the poor. He was suspicious of the ruling class rut. His own life was marked by simplicity and trust in God. He told a story about a man who built bigger barns rather than give to the poor; he asked a rich young man to sell all he had and give to the poor. Systemic poverty will remain until it becomes completely unacceptable to give the name "democracy" to a system that permits unlimited waves of money to flow to the rich, drained out of the economy, and leaving the poor to make it on charity and pittances. We need new prophets who will accept the challenge of making at least three goals realities: (1) revising views on ownership, (2) creating surrogate parenting institutions, and (3) developing a system of guaranteed full employment.

Revising Views on Ownership

It will take prophetic preaching to wake up those who are at ease in Zion and convince them that everything we have belongs to God—our minds, our energy, our land, our food, our water, the sunlight, the reproductive processes, DNA, genetic endowments, the nervous system, and all of the biology, chemistry, and physics that we know. The earth is, indeed, the Lord's and everything in it. And the astute prophet will ever be mindful that those in this country who have old money stole and killed for it. Those with new money used corporate welfare to get it and to keep it. So the new prophets know that those who are well-off can do no less than find an intelligent way of helping those who are least well-off.

Wouldn't it be better to convert a third of our military budget into helping our cities to restore their decaying infrastructure; guarding our parks, swimming pools, and school grounds; providing teacher's assistants in tough schools; supplying more workers for understaffed hospitals and homes for the aged; keeping bathrooms in roadside rest stops clean and well-guarded; building sidewalks and sewers in small rural communities; enabling homebound, non-ambulatory patients to get food, get laundry done, and have safe visits to church, to the mall, and to the voting booth.

There is much to be done. HeadStart, the innovative program designed to provide day care and education for poor, preschool children of working parents, has already reached a million children; it needs to reach another million children. School budgets are tight and playgrounds need attending. We could enhance the quality of life, let those of super-high income carry their fair share, reduce the war-making budget and remove poverty from the face of our society. In the story of the good Samaritan Jesus gave us a view of community that transcends classism and racism. The neighbor is not the one who robs from one who is downtrodden; the neighbor is not the one who is religious. The neighbor is the one who binds up the wounds of the hurt, gives of his own plenty, and privately goes off, not seeking reward.

Creating Surrogate Parenting Institutions

Historically, preachers have been more involved in creating institutions of social uplift, and have depended less upon government intervention to deal with societal ills, than they do today. For Black preachers and congregations, such involvement was understood and necessary. They had to build their own schools, businesses, and organizations to save and empower their people; the government had no interest in the task. With the proliferation of social ills, it is clear that the church and the government are needed for the advancement of our cities. A partnership is needed, not domination by the government. As I have indicated, today's prophets cannot leave politics to the politicians if the politicians' actions further afflict the downtrodden.

A prime opportunity for the church and government to join forces is presented by one of the worst agonies that America has witnessed in the last quarter of a century—children having children. Few things have been so pervasive and will have such a long-lasting negative impact. The prophetic preacher must intervene in this social crisis. Politicians and the government alone cannot be allowed to determine the future of our children, especially children of color and those who are poor and illiterate. Washington has spoken decisively on the issue. Washington's response to these children and their children is to place them on ill-designed welfare rolls, put them in prisons, allow their school systems to deteriorate, or ignore them. Prophets must speak up and step up.

Since the government has determined that we no longer need certain military bases, why hasn't the church asked, What would be a good use for these former bases? I propose that these bases be used to house National Youth Academies. These institutions would serve as *surrogate parenting institutions*. They would be para-school-systems for children who are twelve or thirteen years of age. Targeted for enrollment would be children who are already involved with the juvenile justice system and children whose parents or guardians have shown that they are incapable of properly rearing them. Also included would be children who have been left parentless by AIDS and other tragedies.

These academies would be staffed by teachers and counselors who would be recruited as persons are recruited for the Peace Corps. The government could also aid in this partnership by allowing persons to serve as teachers and counselors to pay off student loans. Such aid would be as appropriate as the G.I. Bill is for veterans. Churches would adopt schools and provide financial and personnel resources.

The curriculum would have a three-faceted design. The first facet would be academic, focusing on just the basics—reading, writing, and arithmetic—in light of modern technology. The second facet would cover human development. This would include making sure that each student develops his or her musical skills, athletic skills, and aesthetic taste, as well as the ability to respect and appreciate others. The final facet of the curriculum would focus on ensuring that all students gain a new practical skill by performing a new job every ninety days. Students would be taught how to prepare healthy meals, fix computers, do basic plumbing, home maintenance, basic car repairs, and so forth.

If Tuskegee College can educate a student for $11,000 a year, National Youth Academies could support a student for no more than *half the cost* of what it takes to incarcerate one juvenile for a year—approximately $35,000.

Developing a Guaranteed Full Employment System

As a nation, we are wealthy enough to have *guaranteed full employment* for everyone, either provided by the government for public services, or subsidized through corporations (or both). A fair tax structure would pay for such employment and the supporting subsidies. Replacing patchwork, stopgap, Band-Aid projects, this system of full employment would include job training, child care, and complete medical coverage. If only one-third of our $300 billion military budget was devoted to this program, its costs would be covered. Would it not be better to have unemployed, low-skilled people doing meaningful and needed work rather than have them home drinking alcohol and using drugs; or stealing for a living; or living on the streets, begging and eating garbage; or living on government dole? Everyone of sound mind and able body should be given honorable work to do, at a decent, living wage. Such a concept will not be easy to sell to people who had a good start in life and, in their comfort, safety, and contentment, fail to understand how anyone could be born in a poor family, how anyone could receive a poor education, how anyone could form weak morals, how anyone could have a low self-concept.

Amos and Micah, the great prophets of the eighth century, shook their contemporaries by declaring God's displeasure with the disparity in economic well-being between the rich and the poor. They cried out for justice and relief for the poor. Martin Luther King Jr. did the same in the twentieth century. For the twenty-first century we must have new prophets who are aware of the gap, aware of the suffering, and who have the intransigence to stand tall and speak in God's name against long-term, systemic, economic greed and indifference. Most likely, this will not be done from the pastorate, but those who go outside the walls must have their efforts buttressed by those who weekly approach the sacred desk.

We do not need socialism. We do not need communism. We do not need any ism. We need to follow the moral principles of the Judeo-Christian revelation of the will of God. They have been so clearly revealed to us by a prophet who specialized in helping the weakest, who took the initiative to turn corrupt systems upside down, and who believed so much in his ministry of service that he laid down his life for it.

NOTES

1. Edward Wheeler, *Uplifting the Race: The Black Minister in the New South 1865-1902* (Lanham, Md.:University Press of America, 1986).

CHAPTER FIFTEEN

William H. Willimon

THE PREACHER AS AN EXTENSION OF THE PREACHING MOMENT[1]

Plato defined good public speaking as a matter of "a good man speaking well." The messenger must be congruent with the message in order for the message to be received. This is particularly true when the message is the gospel of Christ, a message that not only demands to be spoken, but also performed, embodied in the lives of faithful disciples. One of the reasons why Henry Mitchell's preaching impresses us is that in his life he has enfleshed the message he spoke. How well I remember a sermon in Duke Chapel in which Henry and

Ella Mitchell, one as King David, the other as Bathsheba, not only preached a biblical text but, in the deepest sense, *performed* a text, became the text, thus enabling each of us in the congregation to embody the text as well.

We preachers need to hear again the Platonic truth—good speaking involves a good person speaking well.[2] Character, Aristotle's *ethos*, is a prerequisite for faithful preaching.

At the beginning of 1995, *The Christian Century* recapped some of the most significant religious news from 1994. One story was of a number of prominent priests charged with sexual abuse of children. Another told about a major embezzlement case at a large church in the Midwest. Malfeasance at the National Council of Churches. Clergy-laity trysts in Texas. We mainline clergy had snickered when the news was of the sexual shenanigans of TV evangelists, but this was close to home for mainline liberals, and none of us were laughing anymore.

A friend of mine, an economist, was asked to serve on the board of a church charitable organization that helps needy children. His first days on the board were a sort of religious conversion experience for him, so inspired was he by the work of the organization, so impressed was he by the tremendous amount of need. But then he learned of the real salaries of some of the clergy staff. He uncovered accounting irregularities. After prayerful consideration, he brought it to the attention of the directors, and he was dismissed from the board.[3]

He told me, "I think clergy, because they tell themselves that they are doing the work of the Lord, are particularly susceptible to self-deceit. If you're feeding hungry children, none of the moral rules apply to you which apply to other mere mortals."

When we preachers go sniffing about for signs of moral ineptitude, we need look, alas, no farther than the pulpit. My friend Stanley Hauerwas was recently asked about the moral confusion of contemporary clergy. Hauerwas said something to the effect that "you have these people who get out of seminary thinking that their job is to 'help people.' That's were adultery begins." What?

"So you have these clergy," he continued, "who have no better reason for being in ministry than to 'meet peoples' needs.' So little Johnny needs picking up after school. And Johnny's mother, since she is working, calls the pastor, who has nothing else better to do, and asks him to pick up little Johnny. And the pastor thinks, "Well, I'm here to help people." So he goes and picks up little Johnny. Before long the pastor meets a parishioner who is lonely and needs love, and then, when caught in the act of adultery, his excuse is that he is an extremely caring pastor."[4]

I recalled what I thought, at the time, to be a rather silly article in *The Christian Century*, by (who else?) a pastoral care professor, entitled, "Clergy Adultery As Role Confusion." I wondered, What about "Clergy Adultery As *Sin*"? I now see that professor's point. In a culture of omnivorous need and all-consuming narcissism, clergy who have no more compelling motive for their preaching than "meeting peoples' needs" are dangerous to themselves and to a culture without a moral compass.

Certainly, there are many possible sources of clerical moral inepti-tude. We clergy have been encouraged to wallow in the same psycho-therapeutic mire as our people have been—meeting our needs, looking out for number one, if it feels good do it, the relentless feeding of the ego.

I believe that a major source of homiletical renewal is clerical lives grasped by something greater than ourselves: namely, our vocation to speak and to enact the Word of God among God's people. *Clergy ethics has its basis in homiletics*. Morality is not a matter of being unattached to any external determination, free to think and act on the basis of our personal feelings of what is right. Contrary to the beliefs of liberalism, morality is a gracious by-product of being attached to something greater than ourselves, of being owned, claimed, commandeered for larger purposes.[5] That is to say that any account of the moral life begins and ends with the question, Who is the God we worship?

My own moral ineptitude, and its link with my homiletical deficien-cies, was brought home to me a few years ago. Shortly after the war with Iraq, I received a note from one of the older members of my congregation, a note written on light blue stationary, neatly folded, written in a frail, but still lovely hand.

"Have you preached on this particular episode, have you mentioned it in one of your recent sermons? Now that I can't get out and about, I listen on the radio to your sermons, but I do not recall your having mentioned this."

She was referring to a newspaper story (the clipping neatly folded within the light blue envelope) about how American troops had buried alive as many as six hundred Iraqi soldiers in their trenches during a battle. "By the time we got there," one soldier was quoted as saying, "all that was left was hands and arms sticking up out of the sand."

"What does this do to the moral character of our nation?" she asked, in graceful, antique handwriting on the blue note paper. "I grieve for the soul of our country. Where is the moral voice of our clergy in these matters?"

Her words stunned me into renewal of my vocation. The problem, it seemed to me now, was not that I had been too timid in my preaching, too fixated in pop psychology to notice the ethical cataclysm taking place outside our sanctuary, too absorbed with the purely personal problems of my affluent congregation—although I am. My problem was not morality in itself. My problem was that I had not been enough of a preacher to let the Word have its way with me and my preaching. I have worshiped at the wrong altar.[6]

I recalled a wonderful comment by Walter Brueggemann, something said to us preachers, along these lines: "If you are a coward by nature, don't worry. You don't have to be courageous to be a preacher. All you have to do is to get down behind the text. You can say, 'This is not necessarily me saying this—but I do think the text says it.' "

We can hunker down behind the text! Disjoined from service to the text, all I can do is to serve the congregational status quo, run pastoral errands for the world as it is rather than let God use me to create a new world. And that is not only no fun, it's also immoral.

I must make clear in my preaching that I preach what I have been *told* to preach.[7] I serve the text, not those who listen. I must thereby help my listeners recover the adventure of being those who are baptized to listen to the text, those who bear the burden and the blessing of bending our lives in conformity to the demands of Scripture.[8] *Morality is always a liturgical matter; who is the god whom we worship?* Henry Mitchell's honest ruminations on the need for courage in the preacher and the many temptations to cowardice in the ministry are helpful here. Mitchell notes that, particularly among today's youth in the African American community, the preacher who merely wants "success," seeking security and peace at any cost, will not be heard. The preacher must learn to "lean on his Lord" and thus gain the courage to speak to the heartaches and challenges of African Americans in crisis.[9]

In a culture that has lost its moral compass (what we did in Iraq for Exxon has its counterpart in what we are doing to one another in bedrooms), that elderly lady's note on blue stationary called me back to the ethical significance of preaching.

I would like every seminarian in my denomination to read what is, in my opinion, one of the best novels of the late nineteenth century, certainly on of the best novels on the peculiar moral dilemmas of clergy. It is Harold Frederick's *The Damnation of Theron Ware* (1896). It tells the story of a young Methodist preacher who is called to preach, but believes more so that he is called to advance socially through his preaching. Stifled by the confines of petty morality in the midwestern town where he serves, the Reverend Ware longs for a larger stage on which to display his homiletical talents. His best friends—the urbane Father Forbes of the nearby Catholic church; Dr. Ledsmar, the town's one social Darwinian; and Celia Madden, a wealthy connoisseur of the arts—represent all that Ware wants to be in life. The more these friends urge him to sample a social life out of his present reach, the less he regards his own ministerial vocation. His vocation becomes a career, a path up the social ladder through the flattering, eloquent art of his preaching.

Adultery (what is there about us male clergy that makes us so susceptible to this temptation?[10]) is not far behind. When Ware finally confesses his love for Celia, she announces to him that his presumed "improvement" has only served to render a once adequate pastor into a first-class bore. Ware eventually leaves the ministry, victim of his own craving for status and recognition.[11]

Of course, Ware's descent to the level of a rather common adulterer has nothing to do with his inability to meet his personal needs or with his being out of touch with his feelings as a man. His descent is related to his inability to be attached to his vocation as a preacher. When that vocation becomes a mere means to an end, flaws in the preacher's character—which may have been overcome by the preacher's commitment to the ethics of good preaching—are magnified.

Elsewhere I have reflected upon the great fiction of our age, the notion of the person without a role, the idea that we are most fully moral when we have divested ourselves of all external claims upon us.[12] The liberal self, detached from any history, any claim upon the self other than the claims one has personally chosen, does not exist. All of us are busy being determined by something—even the claim that I am living only "for myself" is an externally imposed claim by contemporary American society. So the question is not, "Will I serve some purpose larger than myself?"[13] for freedom from such determination is impossible. The question is, *"Will the master whom I serve be true or false?"*[14]

Preachers are those who are fortunate enough to have our lives caught up in the demanding, never quite finished, wonderful adventure of helping the church to hear God's Word. Aristotle taught that it was too much to expect ordinary people to be good. About the best one could do for ordinary folk was to teach them good habits. Of the three artistic forms of proof that Aristotle listed as available to the public speaker—logos, pathos, and ethos—Aristotle knew the ethos, the character of the speaker "constitutes the most effective means of proof."[15] Every time we stand up to preach, our characters, as they have been formed by the habits required for preaching, prove to the church that it is possible to make very ordinary folk (like preachers) into saints. That is, it is possible even for people who are pathological liars to speak the truth. It is possible for people who are cowards by nature to be so caught up in some project greater than themselves that, despite themselves, they are heroic.

Homiletical habits—disciplined, weekly study, honesty and humility about what the text says and does not say, confidence in the ability of God to make our puny congregations worthy to hear God's Word, a weekly willingness to allow the Word to devastate the preacher before it lays a hand on the congregation—all these are habits, skills of the homiletical craft, which form us preachers into better people than we would be if we had been left to our own devices. This is what Paul meant when he told the Corinthians that it would have been nice if he could have preached to them with flattering, eloquent words, but being a preacher, he single-mindedly "decided to know nothing among you except Jesus Christ, and him crucified" (1 Cor. 2:2 NRSV).

Yes, we live in a culture that has lost its moral compass. Lies are told on the floor of the Senate, in pulpits, and in bedrooms. We pass by the hands and arms sticking up out of the sand without a twitch of conscience. In such a time, it is easy to lose our way. Therefore we preachers would do well to cling to our vocation, to determine to know nothing save Christ and him crucified, to serve the Word before we bow before other gods.

That dear, departed resident alien prophet, William Stringfellow, said it more eloquently than I, with his words, with his life:

> To know the Word of God in the Bible, a person must come to the Bible with a certain naivete, confessing that if God exists at all, God lives independently, though not in insolation, from any one's intelligence, longing, emotion, insight, or interpretations, even those that divine the truth. One must be open to God's initiative, be bereft of all preconceptions. Surrender all initiative. . . . One must take the appalling risk. . . . When a person is so naked, so helpless, so transparent, when one so utterly ceases to try to justify oneself or anyone or anything else, one first becomes vulnerable to the Word of God. . . . When a person becomes that mature as a human being, he or she is freed to listen and at last to welcome the Word. . . . That person is enlightened to discern the same Word of God at work now in the world. . . . Thus is established a rhythm in the Christian's life encompassing intimacy with the Word of God in the Bible and one's involvement with the same Word active in the world.[16]

A good person speaking well. Good preaching is therefore not just a matter of homiletical technique,[17] it is also an issue of character, a moral matter of large proportions. Our chief homiletical-moral task is to be yoked so securely and joyously to the Word that in the process of proclamation of the Word, we become the Word, and it dwells in us richly.

NOTES

1. This chapter is adapted from my article, "Preaching in an Age That Has Lost Its Moral Compass," *The Journal for Preachers* (spring 1995).
2. See Henry Mitchell's classic, *Black Preaching* (New York: J. B. Lippincott, 1970), particularly p. 226.
3. See Randy Frame, "Christian Children's Fund Practices Questioned," *Christianity Today*, 14 November 1994, p. 71; Thomas H. Naylor, "The Trouble With Child-Sponsorship Charities," *The Chronicle of Philanthropy*, 12 January 1995.
4. Hauerwas and I worked on some of these themes earlier in our article "The Limits of Care: Burnout as an Ecclesial Issue," *Word and World* 10, no. 3 (summer 1990): pp. 247-253.
5. I am following an argument here similar to that of Stanley Hauerwas in his article, "Practice Preaching," in the fall 1994 issue of *The Journal for Preachers*. Also see my article, "Why a Pastor Should Not Be a 'Person,'" *Theology Today*, 50 (January 1994). Also see Henry

Mitchell's remarks on the preacher's internalization of the message in *The Recovery of Preaching* (New York: Harper & Row, 1977), pp. 34-35.

6. This woman's exhortation to me, her preacher, illustrates Stanley Hauerwas's assertion that "preaching is not what a preacher does but rather is the activity of the whole community. Preaching as practice is the activity of the church that requires the church to be as able listeners, well-schooled and well-crafted hearers, as the preacher is the proclaimer. Indeed, I suspect one of the great difficulties of preaching in the church today is the preacher's presumption that those to whom they preach do not have ears well-trained to hear. As a result, preaching is not the practice of the community but rather, as it so often is, an exercise in sentimentality" (Hauerwas, "Practice Preaching," p. 57).

    It should be noted that this woman was an eighty-year-old Presbyterian. She had been trained, I presume, to expect something of her preachers and to hold her preacher accountable through her own "preaching" on the light blue notepaper.

7. Again, Hauerwas: "For preaching to be a practice intrinsic to the worship of God requires that the preacher, as well as the congregation, stand under the authority of the Word. That is why preaching should rightly follow a lectionary. . . . [T]he exercise of the ministry of proclamation requires ministers to make clear that the Word they preach is as painful to them as it is to the congregation" (Hauerwas, "Practice Preaching," p. 58).

8. See my *Peculiar Speech: Preaching to the Baptized* (Grand Rapids, Mich.: Eerdmans, 1992).

9. See Henry Mitchell, *Black Preaching* (Philadelphia and New York: J. B. Lippincott, 1970), pp. 225-26.

10. The modern poet, Sisson, in a mock address to John Donne the preacher, ("A letter to John Donne," *The New Oxford Book of Christian Verse*, p. 285), notes a curious relationship between preaching, sex, and ambition:

    . . . the vain, the ambitious and the highly sexed
    Are the natural prey of the Incarnate Christ.

11. For more recent fictional treatments of the moral demise of preachers, see James P. Wind, "Clergy Ethics in Modern Fiction," in *Clergy Ethics in a Changing Society: Mapping the Terrain*, eds. J. P. Wind, R. Burck, P. F. Camenisch, and D. P. McCann (Louisville, Ky.: Westminster/John Knox Press, 1991). I would add to my list of required moral reading for clergy Peter DeVries, *The Mackerel Plaza*, 1958; Nathaniel Hawthorne, *The Scarlet Letter*; John Updike, *A Month of Sundays*, 1974; and Andrew Greeley, *Thy Brother's Wife*, 1982.

12. "Clergy Ethics: Getting Our Society Straight," in *Against the Grain: New Approaches to Professional Ethics*, ed. Michael Goldberg (Valley Forge, Pa.: Trinity Press).

13. George Bernard Shaw writes, "This the true joy in life, the being used for a purpose recognized by yourself as a mighty one; . . . the being a force of Nature instead of a feverish selfish little clod of ailments and grievances complaining that the word will not devote itself to making you happy" (*Man and Superman*, 1903, Epistle Dedicatory).

14. This point is well-argued so well in Stanley Fish's reply to Stephen Carter, "Liberalism Doesn't Exist," *The Duke Law Journal*, 1987, p. 997.

15. Aristotle *Rhetoric* 1.2; see also Richard Lischer, *Theories of Preaching* (Durham, N.C.: Labyrinth Press, 1987), p. 3, who notes how the great homiletical treatises from Augustine through the Middle Ages, as well as the later work of homileticians such as Baxter and Schleiermacher, expend much energy in discussions of the character of the preacher.

16. William Stringfellow, *Count It All Joy: Reflections on Faith, Doubt, and Temptation* (Grand Rapids, Mich.: Eerdmans, 1967), p. 20. Bill Wylie Kellerman has edited a wonderful volume of William Stringfellow's writings, aptly titled *A Keeper of the Word* (Grand Rapids, Mich.: Eerdmans, 1994).

17. Stanley Hauerwas has suggested that ethical theory was devised as an attempt to have ethics without character. Through rules and principles we hope to achieve the good deeds that come, not from right rules and principles, but from good people. There is a sense in which

I believe that homiletical theory and technique, concerns that have so dominated contemporary homiletical thought, may be an attempt to have good preaching without having preachers with the requisite character for good preaching. See also Stanley M. Hauerwas, "Clerical Character," in *Christian Existence Today* (Durham, N.C.: Labyrinth Press, 1988), pp. 133-48.

MARTHA J. SIMMONS is coauthor of *A Study Guide For Celebration and Experience in Preaching* and a contributor to *Sister to Sister: Meditations for and from African American Women.* She practices law in San Francisco, California.

DAVID BUTTRICK is Professor of Homiletics and Liturgics at the Divinity School of Vanderbilt University, Nashville, Tennessee. Among his writings are *A Captive Voice: The Liberation of Preaching, Homiletic,* and *Preaching Jesus Christ.*

FRED B. CRADDOCK is Bandy Distinguished Professor of Preaching and New Testament, Emeritus, at the Candler School of Theology, Emory University, Atlanta, Georgia. Among his writings are *The Luke Commentary, Overhearing the Gospel, Preaching,* and *As One Without Authority.*

ROBERT M. FRANKLIN is Professor of African American studies at Candler School of Theology, Emory University, Atlanta, Georgia, and Program Officer for Rights and Social Justice for the Ford Foundation. He is the author of *Liberating Visions.*

BARBARA HARRIS serves as the Suffragan Bishop of the Episcopal Diocese of Massachusetts.

EDWINA HUNTER is the Joe R. Engle Professor of Preaching at Union Theological Seminary, New York City, New York. She is the coauthor of *And Blessed Is She.*

EUGENE L. LOWRY is the William K. McElvaney Professor of Preaching at Saint Paul School of Theology in Kansas City, Missouri. Among his writings are *The Homiletical Plot*, *Doing Time in the Pulpit*, *How to Preach a Parable*, and *Living with the Lectionary*.

JAMES EARL MASSEY is the former dean of Anderson University's School of Theology, Anderson, Indiana. Among his writings are *Designing the Sermon* and *Movement In Preaching*.

SUSAN D. NEWMAN is pastor of the First Congregational Church of Atlanta, Georgia. She is the author of *With Heart and Hand: The Black Church Working to Save Black Children*.

SAMUEL D. PROCTOR is a faculty member at Duke Divinity School, Durham, North Carolina, and at the United Theological Seminary in Dayton, Ohio. Among his writings are *The Certain Sound of the Trumpet*, *How Shall They Hear?* and *My Moral Odyssey*.

J. ALFRED SMITH SR. is the senior pastor of the Allen Temple Baptist Church, Oakland, California. He is Professor of Preaching and Christian Ministries at the American Baptist Seminary of the West, Berkeley, California.

THOMAS H. TROEGER is the Ralph E. and Norma E. Peck Professor of Preaching and Communications at Iliff School of Theology in Denver, Colorado. Among his writings are *Borrowed Light: Hymn Texts, Prayers and Poems* and *The Parable of 10 Preachers*.

RICHARD F. WARD is Associate Professor of Communication Arts and occupant of the Clement-Muchl Chair at Yale Divinity School, Yale University, New Haven, Connecticut. He is the author of *Speaking From the Heart: Preaching With Passion*.

WILLIAM H. WILLIMON is the Dean of the Chapel and Professor of Christian Ministry at Duke University, Durham, North Carolina. Among his writings are *Sighing for Eden*, *What's Right with the Church*, and *Worship as Pastoral Care*.

PAUL SCOTT WILSON is Professor of Homiletics at Emmanuel College in the Toronto School of Theology, Toronto, Canada. Among his writings are *The Practice of Preaching* and *Imagination of the Heart: New Understandings in Preaching*.

BARBARA BROWN ZIKMUND is president and Professor of American Religious History at Hartford Seminary, Hartford, Connecticut. She is the author of *Discovering the Church* and editor of two volumes on the *Hidden Histories of the United Church of Christ*.